WOODEN TOY
SPACECRAFT

Explore the Galaxy & Beyond with
13 Easy-to-Make Woodworking Projects

Publisher: Paul McGahren
Editorial Director: Matthew Teague
Copy Editor: Kerri Grzybicki
Designer: Lindsay Hess
Layout Designer: Jodie Delohery
Illustrator: Lindsay Hess

Spring House Press
P.O. Box 239
Whites Creek, TN 37189

ISBN: 978-1-940611-83-9

Library of Congress Control Number: 2018965722

Printed in The United States of America

10 9 8 7 6 5 4 3 2 1

Note: The following list contains names used in *Wooden Toy Spacecraft* that may be registered with the United States Copyright Office: Buck Rogers; Cthulhu.

To learn more about Spring House Press books, or to find a retailer near you, email info@springhousepress.com or visit us at www.springhousepress.com.

WOODEN TOY
SPACECRAFT

Explore the Galaxy & Beyond with 13 Easy-to-Make Woodworking Projects

Gonzalo Ferreyra

SPRING HOUSE PRESS

CONTENTS

— 1 —

ICE FIGHTER
8

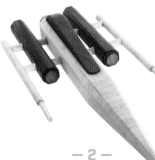

— 2 —

W-WING
22

— 3 —

QUASAR FIGHTER
36

— 4 —

NYDEW 4-EV
50

— 5 —

ZANGOOL SCOUT FIGHTER
62

— 6 —

SKY STATION
76

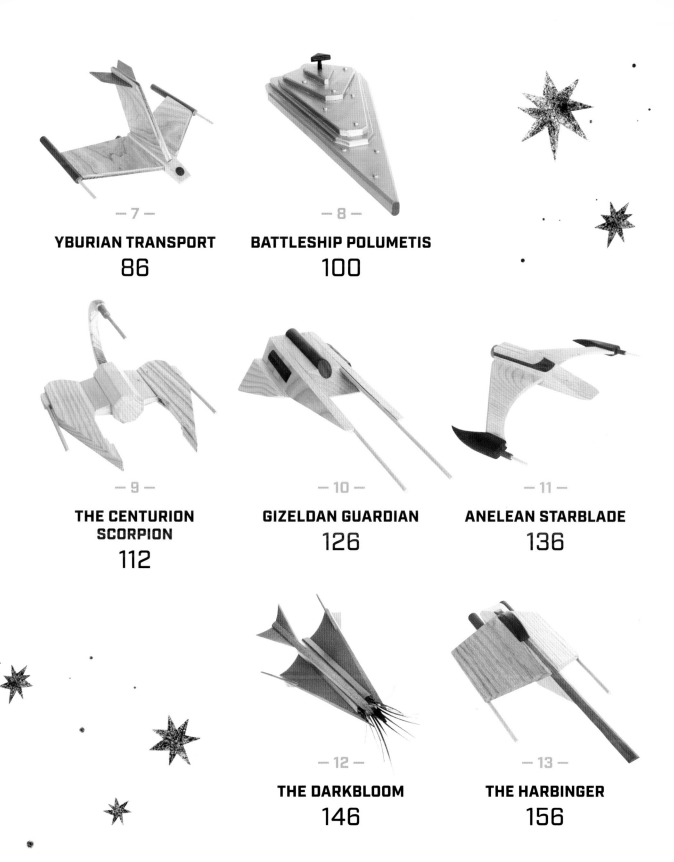

INTRODUCTION

SPACE IS THE NEW FRONTIER.

While we're well into the 21st century, wooden toy vehicle designs have changed little since long before we first landed on the moon: there are plenty of cars, prop planes, trucks, trains, and yes, the occasional Buck Rogers-era rocket, but few projects that hint at the world of the future. This book sets out to change that.

Usually I build furniture—large, practical, ambitious projects that challenge me endlessly and give me the opportunity to develop new skills (or acquire new tools). They call for precise measurements, tricky joinery, and extensive planing, sanding, and finishing. Designing spacecraft allowed me to loosen up a bit. I learned to welcome mistakes and capitalize on them, watching the spacecraft take shape as I cut and re-cut until I was happy with how things looked. I'm pleased to report that many ideas came from staring at a misshapen cut-off or sorting through a scrap bin, an intriguing shape, angle, or curve suddenly pointing me in the right direction.

My goal throughout the writing of this book was simple: each design should be easily completed in a weekend at most (counting finishing), requiring a minimum of challenging set-ups or tools. And yet they should introduce an array of techniques that a woodworker could readily draw on to develop a full range of new designs. The possibilities are indeed endless. If anything, the greatest challenge I faced in putting these projects together was knowing when to stop.

You are, of course, strongly encouraged to improvise freely around the sometimes rigid-sounding steps outlined here. Follow my suggested measurements or ignore them and add an inch here, a ½ inch there. Double the number of guns for a truly fearsome cruiser. Add extra wings or fins. Turn the wings around or tilt them in a new direction. Where I went with a 10° angle, see how it looks at 20°. Play with wood choices to highlight especially cool figuring. Apply a natural oil finish or paint the piece to your liking. Heck, add racing stripes.

But most of all, please have fun in the shop.

Break the rules (but keep it safe).

Experiment.

Welcome your mistakes (well, you can curse them first) and let them inspire you.

You're a woodworker, after all, and what is that if not a high-tech inventor of the future?

A QUICK WORD ABOUT TOOLS

I'm as frustrated as anyone when I pick up a book of woodworking projects and immediately see that it calls for tools I don't own, so while I hesitate to call any tool "indispensable," here are a few that I couldn't have possibly lived without in the making of this book. They're also extremely handy to have for any projects, not just spaceships, so if you don't already own them, either run out and get them (none of these will break the bank) or put them on your next birthday or holiday wish list.

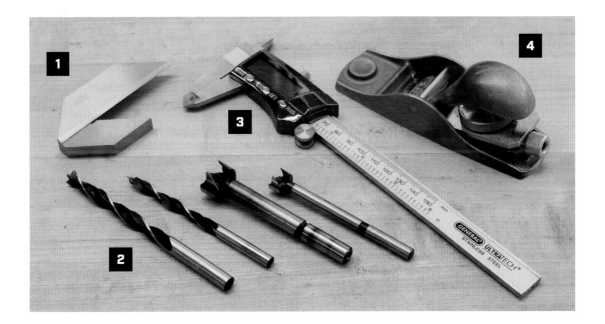

1. Centering square:
There was a time when I didn't know of the existence of a centering square and would awkwardly try to measure centers with a ruler, or worse, by eye. This is especially challenging on the ends of square stock and dowels. Suffice to say that discovering centering squares changed my life. It is a precisely milled, very simple piece of aluminum that gives you a precise center on any square or round stock. You can get one for under $15, so really, there's no excuse.

2. Brad-point and Forstner drill bits:
These are pretty much essential to precision drilling. Lining up the bit point to a mark ensures the hole is where you want it to be; the tip bites into the wood to help eliminate drift. Note that the point protrudes about 1/16 in. beyond the cutting edge and will create a small dimple at the base of the hole; drill too close to the other side and this point will pop through even if the base falls short.

3. Digital calipers:
This is an invaluable tool that will up any woodworker's accuracy game. It's perfect for precise measurement of board widths, dowels, and holes and allows for inside, outside, and depth measurements. There are many inexpensive models available, but I'd suggest you treat yourself to the best you can afford.

4. Block plane:
If by any chance you don't think of yourself as a hand tool person, please make this the one you have in your shop. Mine touches every single piece I make. It's essential for safely creating chamfers, tapering stock, otherwise adding sculptural elements to a piece, and is far more accurate than a tablesaw when you need to adjust a fit. And it's often much quicker, especially given the minimal set-up required. They also feel great in your hand.

ICE FIGHTER

With its classic look and simple build that includes plenty of cool details, the Ice Fighter is the perfect ship to kick things off. Laminating the stock helps define the sleek lines, and the turrets are a distinctive feature that you can (and should) freely deploy for other ships. The large wings are a major part of the ship's look, so make sure to use some nicely figured wood for them.

WHAT YOU'LL NEED

- Tablesaw
- Drill press or handheld drill
- Bench sander or orbital sander
- Bandsaw
- Square
- Block plane
- Pencil
- Spray adhesive
- Wood glue
- Gel cyanoacrylate

- Scissors
- Sandpaper (180, 240, 320 grits)
- Finish or paint(s) of your choice
- Small bar clamp
- ⅜ in. brad-point drill bit
- ¼ in. brad-point drill bit
- Thin-kerf hand saw
- 1 copy of template 1
- 2 copies of template 2

MATERIALS

QTY	PART	DIMENSIONS
2	Fuselage	⅝ x ¾ x 6 in.
1	Fuselage (contrasting stock)	¼ x ¾ x 6 in.
2	Engine dowels	⅜ x 1 in.
1	Wings	5/16 x 4⅜ x 9 in.
1	Cockpit (contrasting stock)	¼ x ⅞ x 2 in.
2	Gun turrets (contrasting stock)	⅜ x ¾ x 1⅞ in.
4	Gun dowels	¼ x 2¼ in.

TEMPLATES: ICE FIGHTER

Copy at 100%

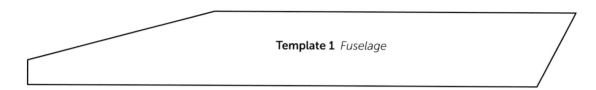

Template 1 *Fuselage*

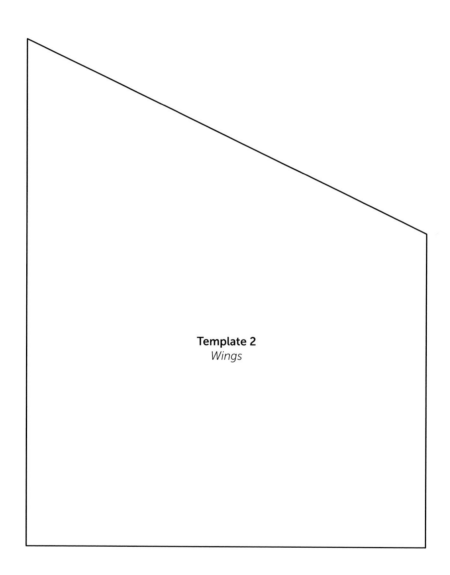

Template 2
Wings

THE FUSELAGE

1 Collect your materials. You'll need one piece of thin ¾ x 6 in. stock and two thicker pieces of ¾ x 6 in. stock in a contrasting color. The thicknesses can vary so long as the total width comes to about 1 ½ in. Shown here are two pieces of ⅝ in. maple and one piece of ¼ in. cherry.

2 Glue it up. Apply wood glue to one side of each of the pieces of thicker stock and sandwich the thin stock.

3 Clamp it up. Clamp the boards using even pressure. You should see a bit of squeeze-out on all sides. Wipe away the squeeze-out with a lightly dampened rag. Let the piece dry for three to four hours.

THE FUSELAGE *(continued)*

4 **Clean it up.** Plane the faces smooth and trim the ends straight to finish with a piece that's ¾ in. thick x 1 ½ in. wide x 6 in. long.

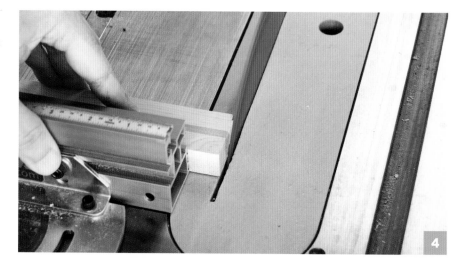

5 **Drill the engine slots.** At the drill press, drill two ⅜ in. holes ¾ in. apart at one end of the piece. The holes need to be about ¾ in. deep so you can insert the engine pipes after tapering the tail. Keep the stock as flat and steady as possible to ensure a straight hole. A square piece of wood makes a good temporary fence to stabilize the piece.

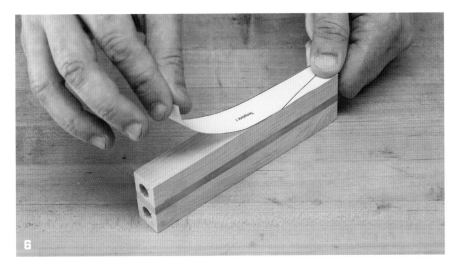

6 **Time for the template.** Copy template 1 and coat the back with spray adhesive. Attach it to the blank, firmly pressing out any air bubbles.

7 **Cut it out.** At the bandsaw, cut close to but not over the template lines.

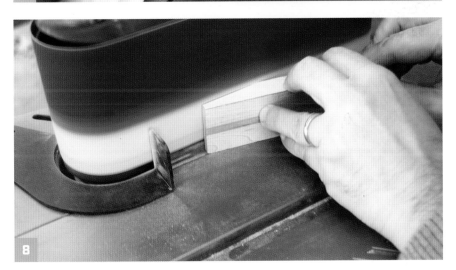

8 **Streamline it.** At the bench sander, remove the bandsaw marks and sand to the template lines. Round the nose and tail.

THE FUSELAGE (continued)

9 **Add the engines.** Drop a small amount of glue into each of the engine bays, insert 1 in. lengths of ³⁄₈ in. dowel, and tap them home.

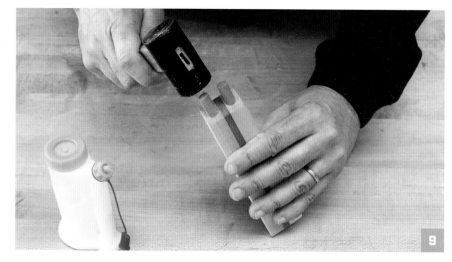

10 **Drill for the base/ hand-hold.** Drill a ³⁄₈ in. hole centered on the underside of the fuselage, ³⁄₈ in. deep. Once the piece is completed, this will allow you to display it on a dowel connected to a small base and will also be perfect for a shorter dowel to hold on to when you fly your piece through space.

11 **Fine-tune it.** With a sharp block plane, lightly chamfer all the edges.

— A NOTE ON DOWEL SIZES —

When you buy dowels for your projects, make sure to confirm the diameters using a set of calipers (see page 7). Many widely available dowels are imported in metric sizes but sold in nominal Imperial measurements, resulting in diameters that will be off by about ¹⁄₆₄ in. When you drill an accurate hole having matched the diameter of the bit to that of the dowel, you'll find that the dowel is loose in the hole, with a notable gap all around. I'd also suggest avoiding dowels simply labeled "hardwood" in favor of those sold by specific species: cherry, oak, or maple. This way you know what you're getting and have a variety of wood grains and colors from which to choose.

THE WINGS

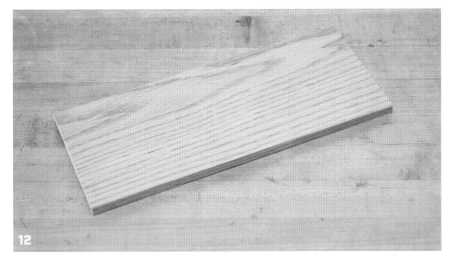

12 **Time to wing it.** You'll need a piece of 5/16 in. stock cut to 4⅜ x 9 in., from which you'll get both wings. Look for attractive figuring (like this piece of oak with some sleek straight grain). Make sure the grain runs along the 9 in. length. This will ensure that when you cut the wings and glue them to the fuselage, you'll have a strong glue-line, long grain to long grain.

13 **Apply the templates.** Glue two copies of template 2 to the board, one at each end as shown.

14 **Bevel the ends.** With your tablesaw blade set to 45°, bevel one end of the piece. Turn it over and repeat at the other end of the piece.

THE WINGS [continued]

15 **Cut them out.** Set your miter gauge for a 25° angle and cut along the template lines (you can, of course, choose to make these cuts at the bandsaw). Cut one wing, turn the piece around, and cut the other wing.

16 **Cut the outside bevels.** Now cut 45° bevels along the short sides of each wing, running the pieces along the fence, so that the bevels are on the tops of the wings.

17 **Cut the inside bevels.** Re-set the blade to 15° and bevel the long edge (the edge that will connect to the fuselage) on the bottom of the wings. A temporary auxiliary fence keeps the sharp beveled edges from slipping into the thin space below your permanent fence.

18 **Mark for the last bevel.** Clamp each wing in a vise with the leading edge facing up and mark a line across the top face of the wing ⅜ in. from the edge, using a square as a guide.

19 **Bevel the edge.** With a block plane, and supporting the back of the piece with your free hand, bevel the edge to create a plane that connects the drawn line with the bottom edge. Don't worry about total precision; you're just looking for a cool aerodynamic bevel.

20 **Streamline the wings.** Sand the pieces, removing the templates and lightly rounding the edges. Avoid the interior edge that will attach to the fuselage. Progress through multiple grits until you reach 320 (I go 180-240-320).

THE COCKPIT

21 On to the cockpit. Mill a ⅞ x 2 in. piece of ¼ in. stock from the same dark wood you used as the center strip of the fuselage—or even better, dig an appropriate piece out of your scrap bin.

22 Bevel the edges. Following the procedure in step 18, mark a line ¼ in. in from each edge on one face of the piece. Clamp the piece in a vise and use a block plane to bevel all four sides of the cockpit at 45°.

23 Mark out windows. With a thin-kerf hand saw, cut shallow lines (two to three light strokes will do it) ½ in. in from each end and lengthwise down the center, cutting first across the top and then extending the cuts down the beveled sides. Attach the small piece temporarily to a larger clamped block to stabilize it, and use your square to keep the cuts straight. Clean up the grooves with the edge of a folded-over piece of 320-grit sandpaper.

THE GUN TURRETS

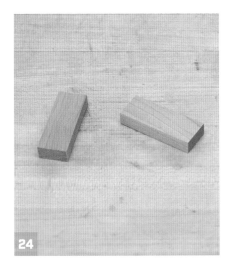

24 **Build the turrets.** Cut two ¾ x 1⅞ in. pieces of ⅜ in. stock from the same dark wood you used as the center strip of the fuselage.

25 **Drill the gun chambers.** At the drill press, drill two ¼ in. holes ½ in. from each end into the front length of each turret. These holes should be ⅜ in. deep.

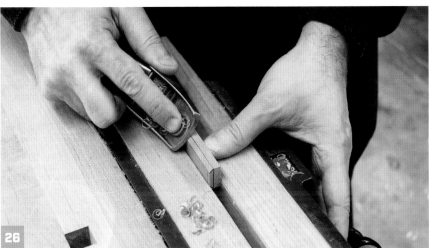

26 **Bevel the turrets.** Following the same procedure as for the cockpit, plane ⅛ in. 45° bevels on all four sides of each turret. Sand each turret up through 320.

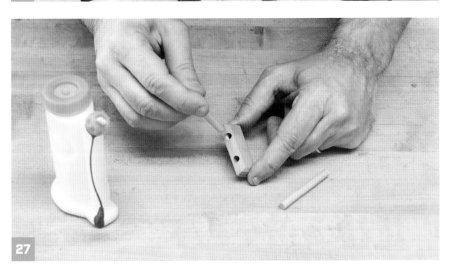

27 **Add the firepower.** Brush a small amount of wood glue into each gun chamber and insert 2¼ in. lengths of ¼ in. dowel. Wipe away any glue squeeze-out with a damp cloth.

THE FINAL BUILD

28 **Final glue-up.** Referencing the photo of the finished fighter, and using the CA-glue clamping trick described on page 84, attach the cockpit to the fuselage and the gun turrets to the wings. Align the turrets on the wings with the help of a square. Attach each wing to the fuselage so it angles down.

29 **Finish it.** Apply the finish of your choice (see page 110 for more on choosing a finish). Natural Danish oil is shown here.

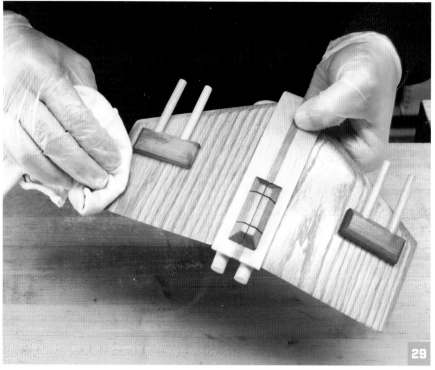

30 **Take flight.** Check around you. Make sure no one is looking. Hold the fighter firmly in one hand. Make whirring noises with your mouth. Lift up the fighter rapidly and move it through the air of your workshop as fast as it will go.

— 2 —
W-WING

The W-Wing is pretty much a study in dowels, but despite its fragile appearance, it is quite sturdy. I was especially pleased with how well the technique of bisecting a dowel worked out. This is also the first appearance of a technique you'll see throughout the book: planing an octagonal shape. It's a terrific way of "rounding" a piece without a lathe, while giving you plenty of surfaces to which you can easily attach other elements.

WHAT YOU'LL NEED

- Tablesaw
- Drill press or handheld drill
- Bench sander or orbital sander
- Bandsaw
- Square
- Block plane
- Pencil
- Spray adhesive
- Wood glue
- Gel cyanoacrylate
- Scissors
- Sandpaper (180, 240, 320 grits)
- Finish or paint(s) of your choice
- ⅜ in. brad-point drill bit
- 5/16 in. brad-point drill bit
- ½ in. brad-point drill bit
- ¾ in. Forstner drill bit
- 2 copies of template 1
- 1 copy of template 2

MATERIALS

QTY	PART	DIMENSIONS
1	Fuselage	1⅛ x 1⅛ x 11¼ in.
1	Exhaust pipe dowel	¾ x ¾ in.
1	Cockpit (contrasting stock)	9/16 x 9/16 x 5¾ in.
2	Fuel tanks (contrasting stock)	¾ x ¾ x 5¼ in.
2	Fuel tank dowels	⅜ x ½ in.
2	Gun dowels	5½ x 5/16 in.
2	Gun dowels	1⅓ x 3/16 in.
4	Interior rod dowels	¾ x 5/16 in.
2	Exterior rod dowels	3 x 5/16 in.

TEMPLATES: W-WING

Copy at 100%

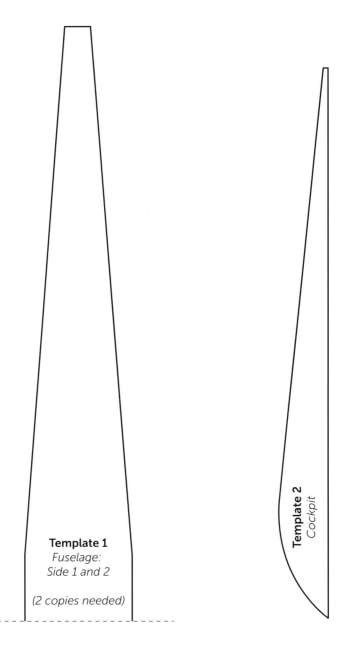

Template 1
Fuselage:
Side 1 and 2

(2 copies needed)

Template 2
Cockpit

THE FUSELAGE

1 Gather some wood. You'll need a 1⅛ x 1⅛ x 11¼ in. piece of stock. If you plan to varnish rather than paint your finished piece, go with a color that matches your dowels to contrast with the wood you'll choose for the cockpit and the fuel tanks.

2 Drill for the exhaust pipe. Using a ¾ in. Forstner bit, drill a centered hole into one end of the piece, ¼ in. deep. If you have a small drill press, drill the hole through a 1 in. length of the same stock for the fuselage to make a simple drilling guide. Clamp to the piece's end and drill through with your hand-held drill; this way the hole will be true. Progress slowly and back out the bit often to free waste.

3 Time for the template(s). Make two copies of template 1. Coat the back of one with spray adhesive and attach it to one side of the blank, aligning the tip with one end of the stock.

4 **Taper the first side.** At the bandsaw, cut the first two tapers, sticking close to the line without going over. Later, you'll plane and sand to final shape.

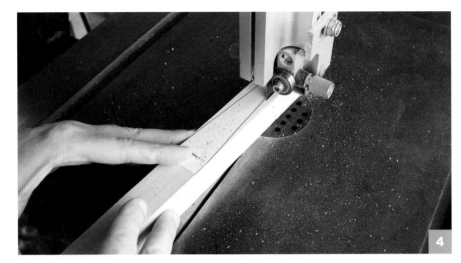

5 **Now for that template again.** Coat the back of the second template 1 with spray adhesive and attach it to the second side of the blank, smoothing the template onto the tapered face you just cut (you may want to smooth this face at the belt sander to make applying the template easier).

6 **Taper the second side.** At the bandsaw, cut the second set of tapers, sticking close to the line without going over. Keep firm downward pressure on the back end of the piece to keep the bandsaw blade from pulling down the tapered face.

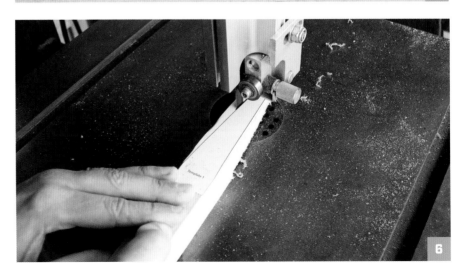

7 **Sand it smooth.** At the bench sander, sand the tapered sides to the line to achieve a sleek rocket shape and remove the templates.

8 **Mark out the octagonal shape.** With a square set to ¼ in. (or just sighting by eye), run a pencil line in from all four edges in both directions of each face (you should have eight lines).

9 **Plane the rocket.** With a block plane, plane to the lines at all four corners to create 45° chamfers. You want a tapered octagonal piece of four wide sides alternating with four narrow sides.

THE FUSELAGE *(continued)*

10 **Drill for the base/hand-hold.** Drill a ⅜ in. hole centered on the underside of the fuselage. I tilted this one slightly so the ship would be in a take-off position once it's on its base.

11 **Add the exhaust pipe.** Glue a ¾ in. length of ¾ in. dowel into the hole.

THE COCKPIT

12 **Mill the blank.** At the tablesaw, trim off a 9/16 x 5¾ in. strip from a piece of 9/16 in. -thick stock.

13 **Cut it out.** Spray the back of template 2 with adhesive and press it down firmly to one side of the blank. At the bandsaw, cut to the line without going over.

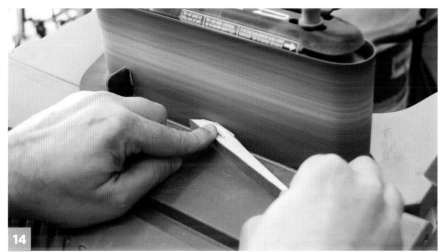

14 **Make it super cool.** At the belt sander, round the front end of the piece and sand away the template until you have a smooth curve. Watch your fingers!

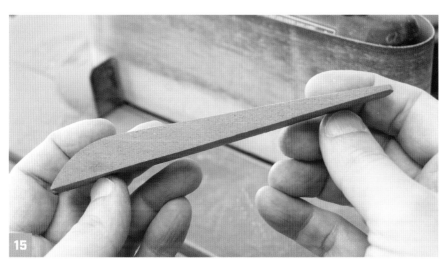

15 **Looking good.** What you want is a long thin piece that widens to a "canopy" shape at one end. If you squint, you should be able to envision the two-man crew in their seats.

16 **Final sanding.** Soften the curve and the edges by hand with some 240-grit sandpaper.

THE FUEL TANKS

17 Collect the material. You'll need two 5¼ in. pieces of ¾ x ¾ in. stock, ideally in a wood that contrasts with that of the fuselage (like these sapele scraps).

18 Drill out the ends. Drill centered ½ in. holes into both ends of both pieces, ¼ in. deep.

19 Mark out the octagons. With a square set to ³⁄₁₆ in. (or just sighting by eye), run a pencil line in from all four edges in both directions of each face (you should have eight lines).

20 Plane to shape. With a block plane, plane to the lines at all four corners, ending with an octagonal shape of eight roughly equal faces.

21 **Sand them smooth.**
Sand each of the faces on a sheet of 240-grit sandpaper laid on a flat surface. Lightly bevel the ends by passing them across the paper three to four times at a 45° angle.

22 **Add snazzy details.**
Glue ³⁄₈ in. lengths of ½ in. dowel into each of the four holes you drilled. Once the glue is dry, trim the protruding dowels at the tablesaw, making sure they're all of even length with ⅛ in. showing.

THE GUNS

23 **Gather the dowels.** You'll need two 5½ in. lengths of ⁵⁄₁₆ in. dowel and two 1½ in. lengths of ³⁄₁₆ in. dowel.

24 **Find the centers.** With a centering square, mark the centers on one end of each of the ⁵⁄₁₆ in. dowels.

25 **Drill some holes.** At the drill press, clamp together two blocks of wood to create a corner against which you'll stabilize the dowels. With a brad-point bit for added accuracy, drill ³⁄₁₆ in. holes ¼ in. into the marked centers of each larger dowel.

26 **Build some firepower.** Dab a small amount of wood glue into each hole and insert the smaller dowels. Set aside to dry.

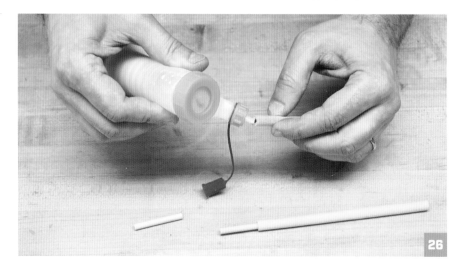

THE FINAL BUILD

27 Mark for holes. With your sharpest pencil, mark two spots 2 in. apart on both sides of the fuselage and two opposing sides of each fuel tank. The rear spot on the fuselage should be 1 in. from the tail, and the rear spot on each fuel tank should be 2⅛ in. from one end. These will all need to line up perfectly, so measure as precisely as possible.

28 Drill for the connecting rods. Set up a ⁵⁄₁₆ in. brad-point bit and drill all your holes ¼ in. deep.

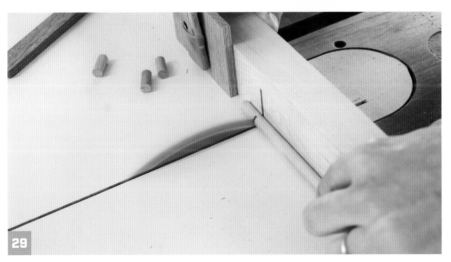

29 Make the interior rods. At the tablesaw, cut four ¾ in. segments of ⁵⁄₁₆ in. dowel. I use a small cross sled with a stop block and a spacer, removing the spacer to keep the small piece from getting caught by the blade.

THE FINAL BUILD *(continued)*

30 **Drill the exterior rods.** At the drill press, lay down a 3 in. length of ⁵⁄₁₆ in. dowel so that the point of the bit touches down at the center of the dowel across its width. Drill through the dowel with a ⁵⁄₁₆ in. bit, bisecting it in two. Repeat this with a second 3 in. piece of dowel, so you have 4 pieces of dowel that end in a ⁵⁄₁₆ in. semi-circle.

31 **Cut to size.** At the tablesaw, trim these ends off at ¾ in. You should have four ¾ in. rods.

32 **Attach the cockpit.** Spread wood glue and a bit of gel cyanoacrylate on the bottom of the cockpit and position it on the top side of the fuselage as shown. Hold firmly in place for 30 seconds until the cyanoacrylate sets.

33 **Glue up the fuel tanks.** Dab a spot of wood glue into each of the holes in the fuselage and insert the four interior rods. Dab wood glue into one set of holes in each fuel tank and attach them to the interior rods.

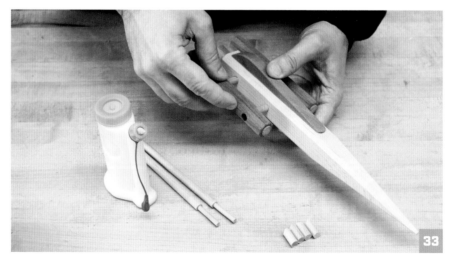

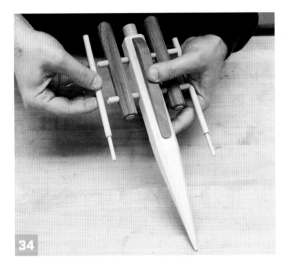

34

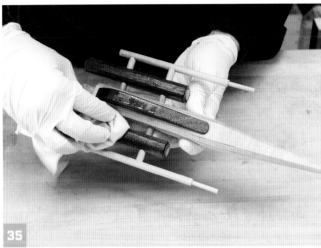

35

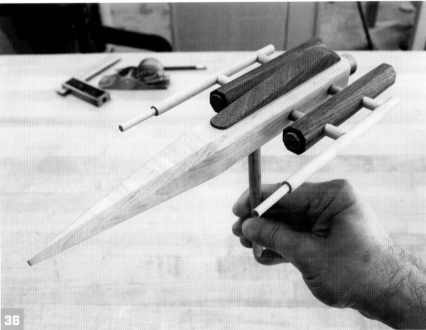

36

34 Glue up the rest. Glue the exterior rods into the outer holes of the fuel tank, aligning them so that the outer semicircles are parallel to each other. Spread a small amount of gel cyanoacrylate into each semicircle and attach the guns, pushing them firmly into the semi-circle and lining them up with each other.

35 Finish it. Apply the finish of your choice, such as Danish oil.

36 Attack the enemy. Lift the fighter off the flight deck (your workbench) with a whirring sound that reaches a roar as you speed it into space (your shop). Rapidly repeat the sound of lasers (*pew-pew* is an excellent choice) as the fighter destroys everything in its path.

— 3 —

QUASAR FIGHTER

This is a classic fighter design and while it's generally a simple build, it does call for a bit of freehand shaping at the bench sander. Follow the images closely and refer frequently to the finished piece for guidance. And of course, as with all the projects, don't worry too much about getting it exactly right. If there's one thing I've learned in compiling this book, it's that there are countless ways to taper and bevel wings for an aerodynamic look. Don't be afraid to adapt as you go and experiment with different angles and curves.

WHAT YOU'LL NEED

- Tablesaw
- Drill press or handheld drill
- Bench sander or orbital sander
- Bandsaw
- Square
- Block plane
- Pencil
- Spray adhesive
- Wood glue
- Gel cyanoacrylate
- Scissors

- Sandpaper (180, 240, 320 grits)
- Finish or paint(s) of your choice
- $3/8$ in. brad-point drill bit
- $5/8$ in. Forstner drill bit
- $1/2$ in. Forstner or brad-point drill bit
- 1 copy of template 1
- 2 copies of template 2

MATERIALS

QTY	PART	DIMENSIONS
1	Fuselage	$3/4$ x 1 x $6^1/2$ in.
1	Cockpit (contrasting stock)	1 x $5/8$ in.
1	Engine dowel	4 x $5/8$ in.
1	Wings	$1/4$ x $4^3/4$ x 6 in.
2	Thruster dowels (contrasting stock)	2 x $5/8$ in.
1	Exhaust pipe dowel (contrasting stock)	6 x $1/2$ in.

TEMPLATES: QUASAR FIGHTER

Copy at 100%

Template 1 *Fuselage*

Template 2
Wings (2 copies needed)

THE FUSELAGE

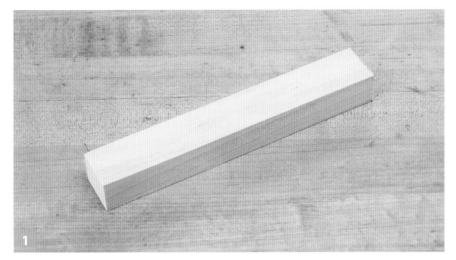

1 Source your material. Chase down a ¾ x 1 x 6 ½ in. piece of stock in the light-colored wood of your choice (like this poplar).

2 Pilot needs a seat. Set your drill press table at 45° and insert a ⅝ in. Forstner bit. Clamp the workpiece to the table and drill a ½ in. deep hole into the 1 in. side of the stock, centered 2½ in. from one end. Proceed slowly, backing out the bit often to free the waste.

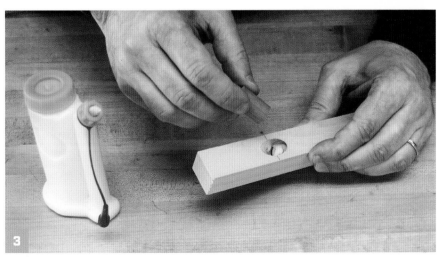

3 Insert the cockpit. Cut a 1 in. length from a ⅝ in. dowel in a contrasting stock. Apply wood glue into the drilled hole, and tap the dowel home. Set aside to dry for one hour.

4 **Trim the excess.** At the tablesaw, trim the cockpit dowel flush with the surface of the fuselage.

5 **Start your engines.** Drill a centered ⅝ in. hole into the end of the piece closest to the cockpit.

6 **Template time.** Spray a copy of template 1 with adhesive and apply to the ¾ in. side of the stock, positioning it so that the cockpit will be on the top side of the fuselage.

7 **Fire up the bandsaw.** Cut to the lines without going over—you can always sand stock away, but you can't stretch a board.

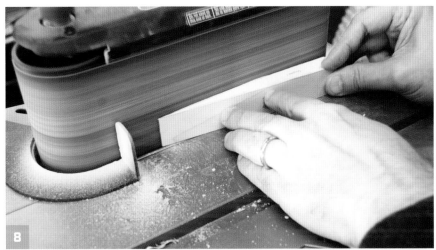

8 **Smooth it out.** Head to the bench sander and sand to the template lines using 240 grit. Smooth the entire piece with an orbital sander or by hand, removing the template.

9 **Add some curves.** At the sander or with a block plane, create a gentle curve from side to side across the entire angled top length of the piece. Lightly chamfer all edges.

THE FUSELAGE *(continued)*

10 **Cut the groove.** With the tablesaw blade extended ½ in. above the surface of the table, cut a saw blade–thick groove 2 in. down the front center of the fuselage. Because of the curve of the blade, the groove will extend further than 2 in. along the underside of the piece; that's okay. Use a push block or scrap piece to hold the piece down and keep your fingers clear of the blade.

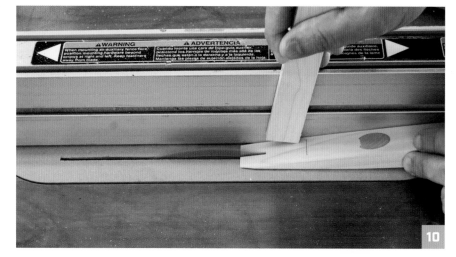

11 **Add the engine.** At the tablesaw, cut one end of a 4 in. length of ⅝ in. dowel at 45° and then trim off this end so you end up with a 1 in. angled piece. Save the rest for another project. Dab the engine hole with wood glue and insert the dowel so the angled face points down.

12 **Drill for the base/hand-hold.** Drill a ⅜ in.-diameter, ¼ in.-deep hole centered on the underside of the fuselage.

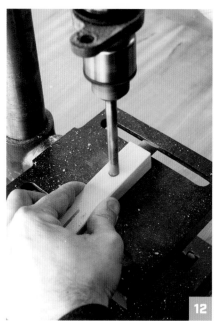

THE WINGS

13 **Select your material.** You'll need one 4¾ x 6 x ¼ in. stock to yield the two wings (like this nicely figured ash). Ideally, the grain should run across the 4¾ in. width for a stronger glue-up.

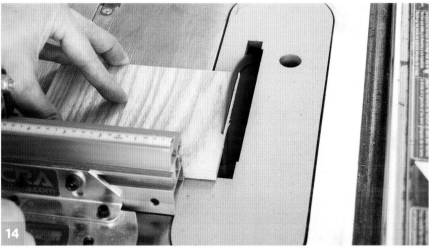

14 **Bevel two edges.** Set your tablesaw for a 20° cut and bevel one of the 4¾ in. edges. Flip the board over and bevel the other 4¾ in. edge (so the bevels are cut on opposing faces).

15 **Apply the templates.** Glue one copy of template 2 to the blank, lining it up to the edge so the resulting wing will angle down and back. Apply a second copy of the template face down to the other side of the blank, positioning it so it doesn't overlap the first template.

16 **Cut them out.** At the bandsaw, cut to the lines (or edges) of the templates without going over.

THE WINGS *(continued)*

17 **Streamline the wings.** At the bench sander, sand to the template lines, removing the bandsaw marks and softening the edges.

18 **Bevel the tips.** Mark a pencil line 1 in. from the outer top of each wing and bevel to this line at the bench sander, sighting by eye and sanding a flat face until the outer edge is ⅛ in. thick.

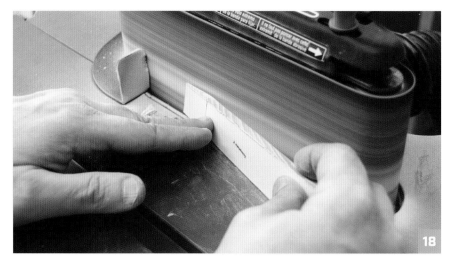

19 **Sand it smooth.** With an orbital sander, remove the templates and smooth to 320 grit.

20 **Bevel the edges.** Back at the bench sander, sand 45° bevels on both faces of each wing (perfect precision isn't important here; you can eyeball the angle so long as you're reasonably consistent).

— WORKING WITH TEMPLATES —

Whenever a step calls for applying a template to a piece of stock, here's the process: copy the template and apply it to the stock with spray adhesive. Lay it down carefully to avoid wrinkles, smoothing out the template with your fingers or the edge of a piece of scrap to remove any air bubbles. Whenever the template is for a piece, such as a wing, that will be glued to another piece, line up the edge that will be glued with a straight jointed (or, in some cases, already chamfered) edge on the stock. Occasionally, you will cut the template to the lines and glue it face down to maintain the proper direction of a beveled edge (say, on the wings).

THE THRUSTERS

21 **Drilling time.** Set up a ½ in. brad-point or Forstner bit on your drill press and drill centered ¼ in.-deep holes into each of two 2 in. lengths of ⅝ in. dowel. Flip the pieces over and drill centered holes ¹⁄₁₆ in. deep (these won't have dowels inserted into them). Hold the pieces firmly and take care to keep the holes centered.

THE THRUSTERS *(continued)*

22 Angle the exhaust pipes. Set your tablesaw blade at 45° and cut the angle at both ends of a 6 in. length of ½ in. dowel.

23 Cut to size. At the tablesaw, trim off these angled ends at ½ in. (you're just using the ½ in. angled pieces; save the rest for another project). Proceed slowly to keep the piece from flying off into space.

24 Glue it up. Dab a bit of wood glue into the ¼ in.-deep holes and insert the angled ½ in. dowels with the bevel facing the underside of the ship as shown. There you have it: warp speed (sure, they kind of look like lipsticks, but trust me).

THE GUNS

25 **Make the guns.**
The goal here is to create a flat surface along 1 in. of each dowel for a stronger glue-up when you attach it to the wing. Set the blade of your tablesaw a scant 1/64 in. above the surface and set a stop 1 in. from the blade. Slowly, keeping the dowel from turning, push the dowel over the blade until it hits the stop, and back. This can be accomplished right on the table with a miter gauge, but is much easier (and safer) with a cross sled, as shown.

THE FINAL BUILD

26 **Attach the guns.**
Working with one gun at a time, spread a thin line of gel cyanoacrylate along the flattened length of each dowel and attach it to the outer edge of the wing, sandwiching it with one on top and one below.

THE FINAL BUILD (continued)

27 Attach the wings. Working on one wing at a time, spread a thin line of wood glue along the interior beveled edge of each wing, add a few dots of gel cyanoacrylate, and attach it to the fuselage about ⅛ in. from the top of the fuselage and ⅛ in. from the rear. Use a straight edge to line up the wings.

28 Attach the thrusters. Dry-fit the thruster to the wing at the bottom where the wing meets the fuselage and lightly mark where the thruster touches the wing. Spread thin lines of gel cyanoacrylate along that mark and along the chamfered edge of the fuselage parallel to the mark. Attach the thrusters with the exhaust pipes pointing down (like the fuselage engine exhaust) and with ⅛ in. of the thruster forward of the wing.

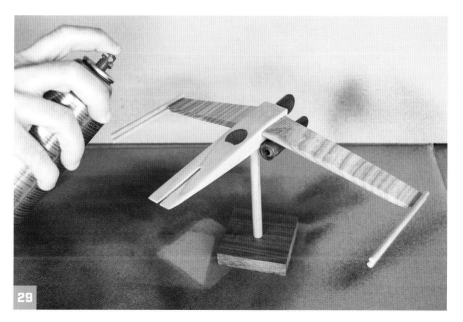

29 Apply the finish.
For something a little different, this one has three coats of spray satin poly, lightly sanded between coats with 320 grit. After sanding, remove any sanding dust with a tack cloth.

30 Go to warp speed.
Hold the Quasar Fighter firmly in mid-air and move it steadily through space. Suddenly, push it forward as fast as you can, loudly making a sound that's somewhere between a whoosh and a boom.

— 4 —
NYDEW 4-EV

While ornamentation is generally avoided in these projects in the interest of keeping things simple and allowing each maker free reign, I really like the circle pattern on this one, which evokes the small planetary system of which Nydew is the largest and friendliest planet. Make sure you use a sharply contrasting wood color so it really stands out. And take your time refining the wings, which are key to the ship's elegant, streamlined shape.

WHAT YOU'LL NEED

- Tablesaw
- Drill press or handheld drill
- Bench sander or orbital sander
- Bandsaw
- Square
- Block plane
- Pencil
- Spray adhesive
- Wood glue
- Gel cyanoacrylate
- Scissors
- Sandpaper (180, 240, 320 grits)
- Finish or paint(s) of your choice
- 5/8 in. Forstner drill bit
- 3/16 in. brad-point drill bit
- 1/4 in. brad-point drill bit
- 3/8 in. brad-point drill bit
- 1/2 in. Forstner or brad-point drill bit
- 1 copy each of templates 1 and 2
- 2 copies of template 3

MATERIALS

QTY	PART	DIMENSIONS
1	Fuselage	$7/8$ x $1\frac{1}{4}$ x $7\frac{1}{2}$ in.
1	Cockpit dowel (contrasting stock)	$1/2$ x $5/8$ in.
1	Fuselage dowel (contrasting stock)	$1/4$ x $3/16$ in.
1	Fuselage dowel (contrasting stock)	$1/4$ x $1/4$ in.
1	Fuselage dowel (contrasting stock)	$1/4$ x $1/2$ in.
1	Fuselage dowel (contrasting stock)	$1/2$ x $1/2$ in.
1	Wing elevators	$1/4$ x $1\frac{3}{4}$ x 6 in.
1	Wings	$3/8$ x $4\frac{1}{2}$ x 12 in.
2	Small gun dowels (contrasting stock)	6 x $3/16$ in.
1	Large gun dowel (contrasting stock)	6 x $1/2$ in.

TEMPLATES: NYDEW 4-EV

Copy at 100%

Template 3
Wings

Template 1
Fuselage: Side 1

Template 2
Fuselage: Side 2

THE FUSELAGE

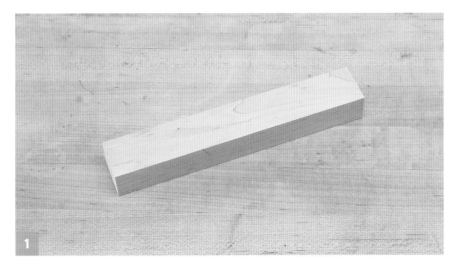

1 **Source materials.** You'll need a 1¼ x ⅞ x 7½ in. piece of stock in the light-colored wood of your choice. The grain should run along the 7½ in. length.

2 **Mark for drilling.** Mark for centered (across the width) holes along the top of the fuselage at the following distances from the front end: 1¼ in., 2⅜ in., 2¾ in., 3³⁄₁₆ in., and 3¾ in.

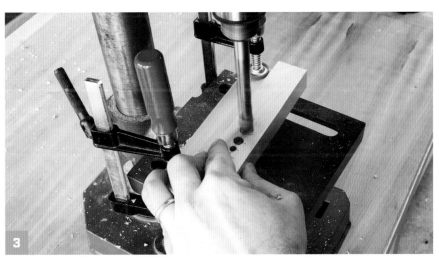

3 **Drill some holes.** Using a ⅝ in. Forstner bit, drill a ½ in.-deep hole at the 1¼ in. mark (this will be the cockpit). Drill the other marks ¼ in. deep and sized as follows: ³⁄₁₆ in. hole at the 2⅜ in. mark; ¼ in. at 2¾ in.; ⅜ in. at 3³⁄₁₆ in.; and ½ in. at 3¾ in. Set up a temporary fence to ensure the holes line up along the center of the piece.

THE FUSELAGE

4 **Cut the dowels.** Start with dowels in a contrasting stock. At the tablesaw, cut a ½ in. length of ½ in. dowel, and ¼ in. lengths of ³⁄₁₆ in., ¼ in., ³⁄₈ in., and ½ in. dowels (make the cuts a scant ¹⁄₆₄ in. oversize to ensure they reach full depth and sand them flush). Proceed slowly to keep from sending the small pieces into deep space.

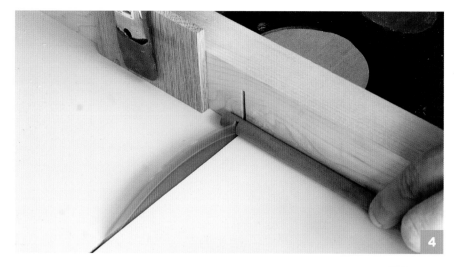

5 **Glue them in.** Dab wood glue into each of the holes and insert the respective sized dowel. Set aside to dry.

6 **Apply the first template.** Glue template 1 to the ⁷⁄₈ in. face of the block, lining up the front with the cockpit end of the block.

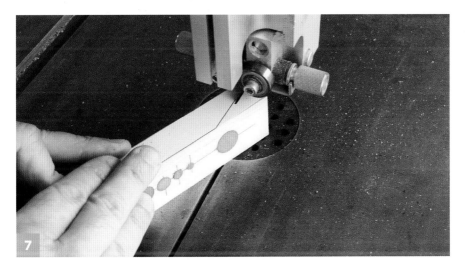

7 **Cut it out.** At the bandsaw, cut close to the template lines without going over.

8 **Apply the second template.** Cut template 2 in half along the narrow width and glue the two pieces to the ends of the 7/8 in. face of the block, lining up the front with the cockpit end of the block and smoothing it down onto the newly cut front angle.

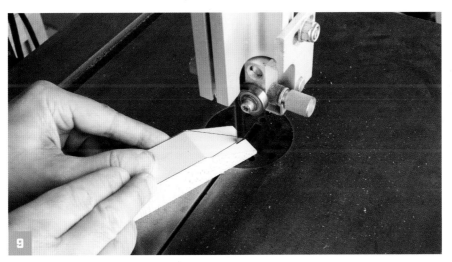

9 **Cut it out.** At the bandsaw, cut close to the template lines without going over.

THE FUSELAGE *(continued)*

10 **Sand it smooth.** At the bench sander or with an orbital sander, smooth the entire fuselage, removing the templates, eliminating saw marks, and sanding the dowels flush. Round the edges and points for a sleek, state-of-the-art fuselage.

11 **Make the elevators.** "Elevators" are those little side wings off the tail you see on many aircraft. At the tablesaw, first set your miter gauge to 15° and cut the angle at both ends of a 6 x 1¾ x ¼ in. piece of stock (note that 6 in. of stock is more than you'll need, but it'll allow for safer cuts).

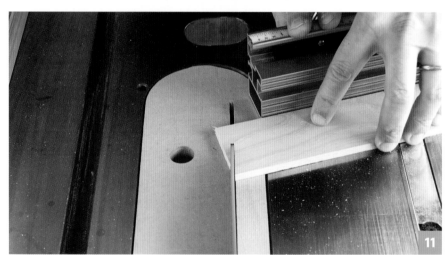

12 **Now for the second cut.** Adjust the miter gauge to 30° and cut at both ends to produce two sharp pointed triangles with a ½ in. base. To make the rudder, adjust the miter gauge back to 15° and trim off one end of the piece to create a third triangle of the same size and shape as the two you already cut.

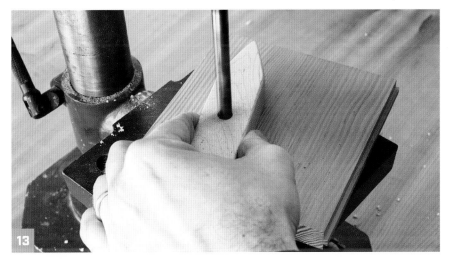

13 **Drill for the base/ hand-hold.** Drill a ⅜ in. hole centered on the underside of the fuselage, ⅜ in. deep.

14 **Glue it up.** Dab a few dots of gel cyanoacrylate on each of the elevators and attach them to each side of the tail as shown, using a square to ensure the elevators are lined up with each other. Do the same with the rudder. Set the whole thing aside to dry while you tackle the wings.

THE WINGS

15 **Source your stock.** Start with a 4½ x 12 in. piece of ⅜ in. stock. I grabbed one of the many spare pieces of oak I have tucked around the shop and milled it to size.

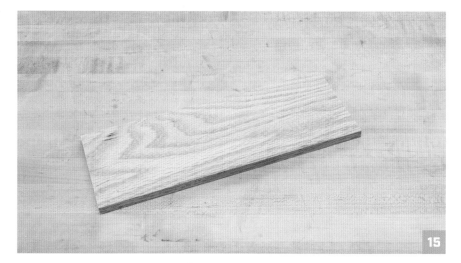

16 **Apply the templates.** Glue two copies of template 3 to the board. Arrange them as shown so they offset and minimize wood waste.

17 **Cut them out.** At the bandsaw, cut out both wings, hewing to the template line without going over. Make the cuts as close as possible with a standard ½ in. blade or install a narrow blade to cut the tight inside corners. Finish rounding the corners as part of the next step.

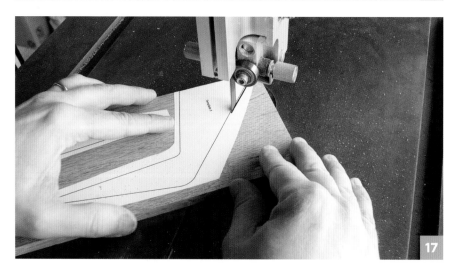

18 **Head to the bench sander.** Sand to the template lines, removing the bandsaw marks and creating a sleek curve that narrows to a fine tip at the back. Chamfer the edges at 45° by eye.

THE GUNS

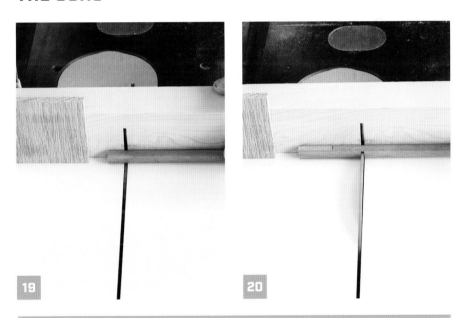

19 **Flatten part of each dowel.** Set your tablesaw blade a scant $\frac{1}{32}$ in. above the surface. Supporting the stock with a cross sled positioned so the stock meets the top arc of the blade, push one end of two 6 in. lengths of $\frac{3}{16}$ in. dowel across the blade, flattening a $1\frac{1}{8}$ in. length on each (set a stop). Repeat with the other ends of the dowels, and then repeat this whole process with a 6 in. length of $\frac{1}{2}$ in. dowel. As in step 11 of this project, the 6 in. length is more than you need, but allows for safer cuts.

— SANDING —

Throughout the projects, I point you over to a bench sander at some point, usually right after you cut out a piece at the bandsaw. If you don't have a bench sander, don't despair (although this may be a good time to get yourself one; my inexpensive one is a workhorse in the shop). You can certainly achieve reliable results with a block plane, handheld sander, or simply with sandpaper. I suggest 240 grit at the bench sander, working up to 320 for a final smoothing by hand.

20 **Cut them to size.** At the tablesaw, cut a 2 in. length from each end of the $\frac{3}{16}$ in. dowels and each end of the $1\frac{1}{2}$ in. pieces.

THE FINAL BUILD

21 **Attach the wings.** Working with one at a time, spread wood glue along the inside edge of each wing. Wipe away two spots about an inch apart and add a dot of gel cyanoacrylate. Attach it to the side of the fuselage so the front edge is about ⅛ in. back from the beginning of the nose taper and hold it firmly in place for 30 seconds.

22 **Attach the large guns.** With a square set at 2¼ in. and braced against the fuselage, attach each ½ in. dowel, spreading cyanoacrylate along the flat edge and pressing to the wing bottom, with the flat length of dowel fully attached to the wing (this also serves as a guide to ensure it extends out the correct distance). Hold in place for at least thirty seconds, or until set. As shown, set the piece on a small block to make room for the rudder and keep the ship stable.

23 **Attach the small guns.** Apply cyanoacrylate to glue the 3/16 in. dowels to the underside of each wing, staggered 1 in. apart (a spacer helps) and protruding 7/8 in.

24 **Apply finish.** Make the details on the fuselage really pop.

25 **Circle the planet.** Bring the 4-EV into orbit around its native planet, swinging in a wide arc as it closes in and comes to a soft landing.

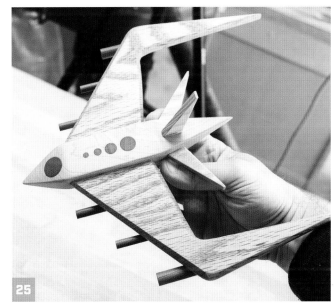

— 5 —
ZANGOOL SCOUT FIGHTER

Thanks to its relatively small size and the sleek aerodynamics made possible by the long nose and tucked-back wings, the Scout is widely acknowledged to be one of the fastest, most agile fighters in the universe. I think the overall look evokes some of the spacecraft that visionaries of the fifties thought we'd all be flying by now. Note that for the first (but certainly not last) time in this book, we'll be using a router, in this case to create shallow mortises to strengthen the thin wing connectors.

WHAT YOU'LL NEED

- Tablesaw
- Drill press or handheld drill
- Bench sander or orbital sander
- Bandsaw
- Square
- Block plane
- Pencil
- Spray adhesive
- Wood glue
- Gel cyanoacrylate
- Scissors
- Sandpaper (180, 240, 320 grits)
- Finish or paint(s) of your choice
- Mallet
- $3/8$ in. brad-point drill bit
- $3/16$ in. brad-point drill bit
- Router and router table
- $1/8$ in. straight router bit
- 1 copy each of templates 1, 2, and 3
- 2 copies of template 4

MATERIALS

QTY	PART	DIMENSIONS
1	Fuselage	$3/4$ x $1^{3}/_{16}$ x $6^{1}/_{2}$ in.
1	Cockpit dowel (contrasting stock)	$1^{1}/_{4}$ x $3/4$ in.
1	Exhaust pipe dowel (contrasting stock)	2 x $3/8$ in.
1	Nose	$2^{1}/_{2}$ x $3/16$ in.
1	Fin (contrasting stock)	$1/8$ x 1 x 3 in.
2	Wings	$1/2$ x $3/4$ x $5^{1}/_{2}$ in.
1	Wings	$1/8$ x $1^{1}/_{4}$ x $7^{1}/_{4}$ in.
2	Gun dowels (contrasting stock)	$3^{1}/_{2}$ x $1/4$ in.

TEMPLATES: ZANGOOL SCOUT FIGHTER

Copy at 100%

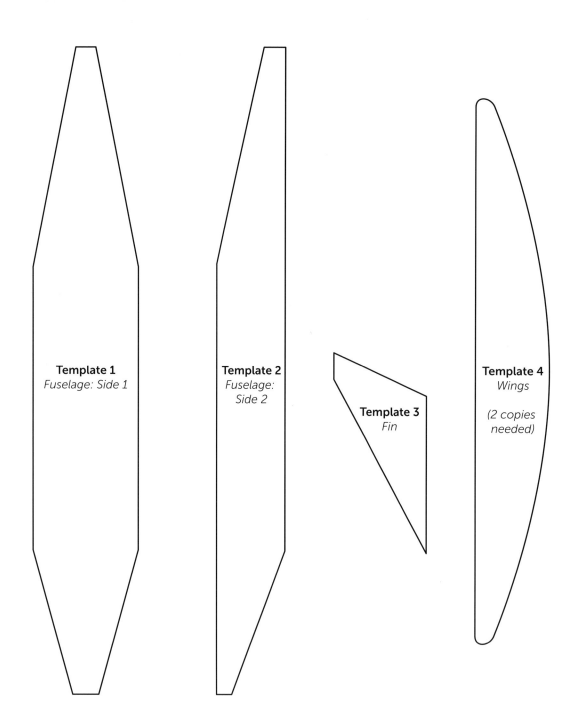

Template 1
Fuselage: Side 1

Template 2
*Fuselage:
Side 2*

Template 3
Fin

Template 4
Wings

*(2 copies
needed)*

THE FUSELAGE

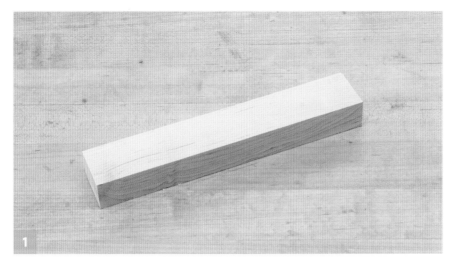

1 Source material. You'll need a piece of ¾ x 1³⁄₁₆ x 6½ in. stock in the wood of your choice, with grain running the long way.

2 Drill for the cockpit. Drill a ⅜ in. hole all the way through the ¾ in. face of the stock, 1¼ in. from one end of the stock and with its center ⁷⁄₁₆ in. from the top. Use a backer board underneath the stock to reduce tear-out.

3 Insert the cockpit dowel. Cut a 1¼ in. length of ⅜ in. dowel in a color that will contrast with your fuselage material and glue it into the hole with a dab of wood glue. You may need to tap it with a mallet to work it all the way through the piece. Don't worry if the ends protrude a bit; we'll take care of that soon.

THE FUSELAGE *(continued)*

4 **Drill for the exhaust.** At the drill press, drill a ⅜ in. hole into the end furthest from the cockpit. It needs to be centered across the 1³⁄₁₆ in. face of the stock and ½ in. from the top face (the face with the dowel/cockpit). Make the hole a full 1¼ in. deep, backing out the bit periodically and stabilizing the piece against a square block.

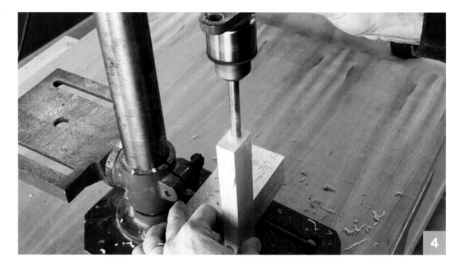

5 **Drill for the base/hand-hold.** Drill a ⅜ in. hole ⅜ in. deep on the underside of the fuselage, centered across the width and 4 in. from the front end of the piece.

6 **Drill for the nose.** Change out your bit and drill a ³⁄₁₆ in. hole into the opposite end from where you just drilled for the exhaust, with the hole again centered across the 1³⁄₁₆ in. face, but in this case ⅛ in. from the bottom face.

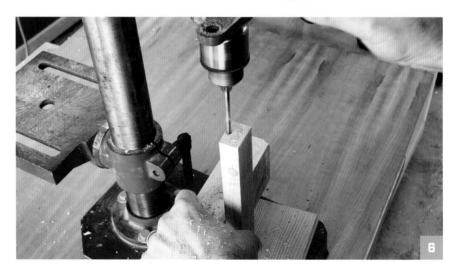

7 **Grab template 1.** Spray the template with adhesive and apply it centered on the 1³⁄₁₆ in. face. Make sure that the longer taper is lined up with the front (cockpit) end of the piece.

8 **Head to the bandsaw.** Cut close to the template lines without going over. Keep an eye on the nose; the cut should leave you with the drilled hole at the very end of the taper. These and the next set of templated cuts will fully reveal the cockpit.

9 **Grab template 2.** Cut template 2 in half along the narrow width and glue the two pieces to the ends of the ³⁄₄ in. face of the block, lining up the longer taper with the cockpit end of the block and smoothing it down onto the newly cut front angle.

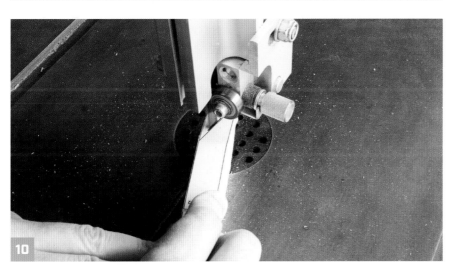

10 **Back to the bandsaw.** Cut close to the template line without going over. Again, watch that nose so you don't drift into the drilled hole. On the engine end, you will cut into the drilled hole just a bit; that's fine.

THE FUSELAGE *(continued)*

11 **Refine the shape.** At the bench sander, smooth the piece using 240 grit, then give it a final sanding by hand, rounding all the edges until the fuselage is as sleek as you want it to be.

12 **Add the exhaust pipe.** Cut a 2 in. length of ⅜ in. dowel and glue it into the tail end of the fuselage.

13 **Add the nose.** Cut a 2½ in. length of ³⁄₁₆ in. dowel and glue it into the hole at the front end of the fuselage.

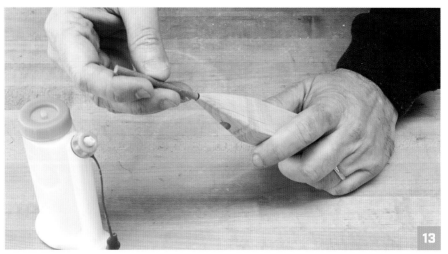

14 **Build a fin.** Spray template 3 with adhesive and apply it to a ⅛ x 1 x 3 in. piece of stock (more than you need, but will help keep you fingers away from the blade), arranging the template so the grain runs the long way. At the bandsaw, cut along the lines without going over. Use a push-stick to keep your fingers away from the blade as you cut this small piece.

15 **Refine the fin.** At the bench sander or by hand, sand the fin to the template, removing the bandsaw marks and the template.

16 **Bevel the edges.** Holding the stock in a bench vise, and with a block plane, bevel the front and top edges (but not the bottom edge) on both sides at 45° to create a slightly sharpened edge. Set the fin aside until final glue-up.

THE WINGS

17 Source the materials. The wings are composed of two sections, for which you'll need two pieces of ¾ x ½ x 5½ in. stock and one piece of ⅛ x 1¼ x 7¼ in. stock.

18 Cut out exterior sections. Glue two copies of template 4 to the two pieces of ¾ x ½ x 5½ in. stock. At the bandsaw, cut to the lines without going over.

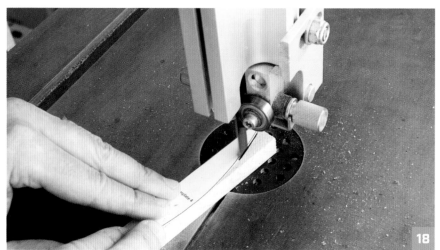

19 Refine the curves. Sand to the lines, round the shape, and remove the templates at the bench sander with 240 grit. Set the pieces aside.

20 **Cut interior sections.** Set the miter gauge of your tablesaw to 30° and cut the end of the 1/8 x 1 1/4 x 7 1/4 in. piece of stock. With the gauge still at 30°, cut two 2 1/2 in. long pieces.

21 **Grab your block plane.** Lightly bevel the front and back edges at 45°, sighting by eye, to create a more streamlined shape. Remember, this fighter needs to cut through space at light-speed plus.

THE FINAL BUILD

22 **Set up the router.** Insert a ⅛ in. bit into your router and the router into your router table. Adjust the fence so it's ³⁄₁₆ in. from the interior edge of the bit. Adjust the bit height to cut a ⅛ in. deep dado.

23 **Mark the fence.** With the help of a square, mark the reach of the bit on both sides of the cutting edge, as precisely as possible on the fence (or clamp on a temporary wooden fence and make your marks on that).

24 **Mark the fuselage.** Make parallel pencil marks on both sides of the fuselage where the front taper flattens out and again 2½ in. back from this point. With a square, extend the marks across the top and bottom sides of the piece.

25 **Mark the outer wings.** Make pencil marks on the flat side of each outer wing piece, 2½ in. from one end. With a square, run this line across the other three sides of the piece.

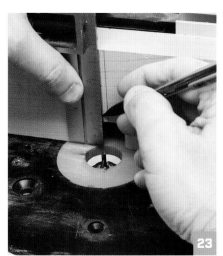

26 **Rout the fuselage dadoes.** Run the fuselage right to left along the fence, dropping down slowly so the first mark lines up with the leftmost fence mark. Lift it away as the second line reaches the rightmost mark. Use push sticks. Rout both sides, making sure you reference both from the top face. Adjust the fence to widen the dado so the interior wing pieces fit snugly into the dadoes.

27 **Rout the wing dadoes.** Run the first (left) wing along the fence up to the mark and lift it away. Drop the second (right) wing onto the bit and run it through to the outer edge. Again, make sure you reference from the top face of each wing. Watch your fingers! Adjust the fence as necessary to widen the dado so the interior wing pieces fit snugly into the dadoes.

28 **Attach the interior wings.** Working one side at a time, run a thin bead of wood glue along the fuselage dadoes and add two dots of gel cyanoacrylate. Insert the wing panes and push them home. If the fit isn't snug enough, hold the piece in place for thirty seconds or so until the cyanoacrylate takes hold.

THE FINAL BUILD (continued)

29 **Attach the exterior wings.** Repeat the process to glue on the exterior wing sections.

30 **Attach the fin.** Spread a thin line of gel cyanoacrylate along the bottom edge of the fin and attach it to the top of the fuselage, centered about 1/8 in. from the rear.

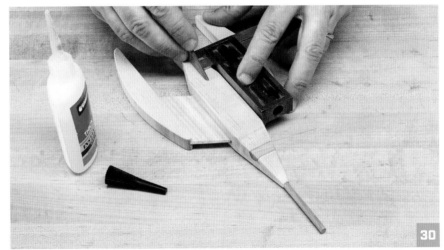

31 **Attach the guns.** Apply cyanoacrylate to glue two 3½ in. lengths of ¼ in. dowel to the undersides of the wing attachments as shown.

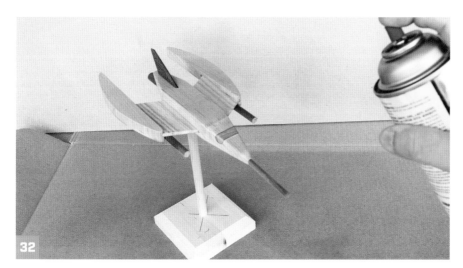

32 Apply finish.
Apply the finish of your choice, such as with three coats of satin poly, lightly sanded with 320 grit between coats.

33 Find out what this baby can do.
Approach the planet Zangool's exosphere at moderate speed, hit the afterburners, and feel those g-forces as you enter interplanetary space.

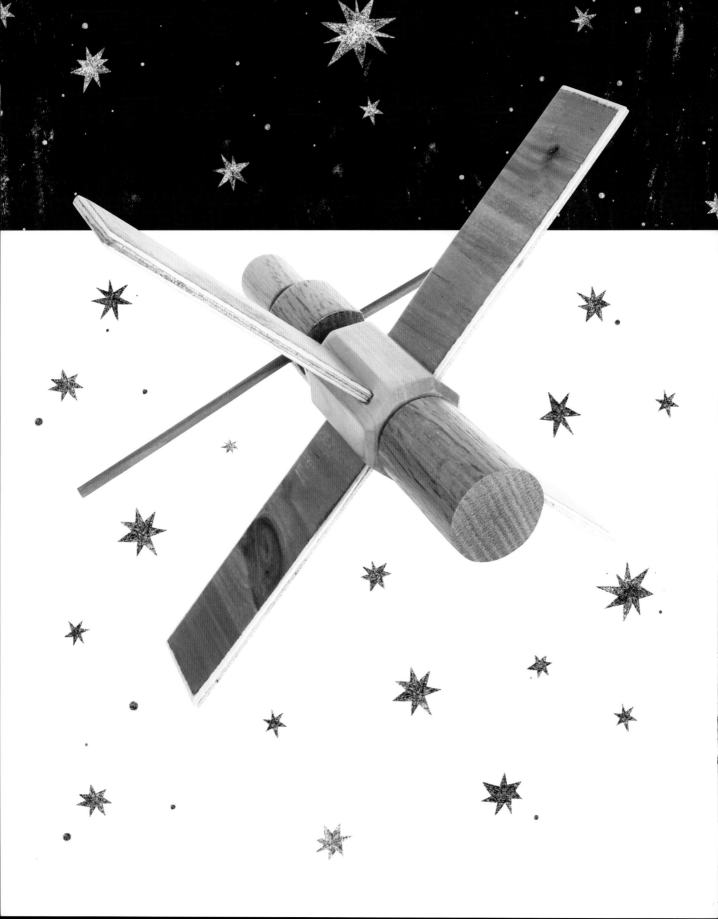

SKY STATION

We take a brief foray into the real world for this project that is inspired by our national history of space exploration. Take extra care keeping your pieces straight as you drill holes into the pieces for the dowels. Any misalignment will appear all too clearly in what is essentially a straight row of connected modules. And while you can certainly mill solid wood for the solar panels, I encourage you to use plywood, which adds depth and texture thanks to the exposed interior layers.

WHAT YOU'LL NEED

- Tablesaw
- Drill press or handheld drill
- Bench sander or orbital sander
- Bandsaw
- Square
- Block plane
- Pencil
- Spray adhesive
- Wood glue
- Gel cyanoacrylate
- Scissors
- Sandpaper (180, 240, 320 grits)
- Finish or paint(s) of your choice
- Scrap wood, 1⅛ in. wide
- Small bar clamp or vise
- Straight edge
- Router and router table
- ⅛ in. straight router bit
- ½ in. brad-point drill bit
- ³⁄₁₆ in. brad-point drill bit
- ⅜ in. brad-point drill bit

MATERIALS

QTY	PART	DIMENSIONS
1	Service module dowel (section 1)	1½ x 1 in.
1	Command module dowel (section 2)	1⅜ x 1½ in.
1	Central unit (section 3)	1½ x 1½ x 2¼ in.
4	Solar panels	¼ x 1½ x 4½ in. plywood
1	Orbital workshop dowel (section 4)	2 x 1¼ in.
1	Connector dowel	½ x ½ in.
2	Connector dowels	⅞ x ½ in.
1	Connector dowel	⅝ x ½ in.
2	Connector dowels	4¼ x ³⁄₁₆ in.

BUILD THE MODULES

1 **Build the service module—section 1.**
Cut a 1½ in. length of 1 in. dowel and set it aside for use later in the project.

2 **On to the command module—section 2.**
Cut a 1⅜ in. length of 1½ in. dowel and set it aside.

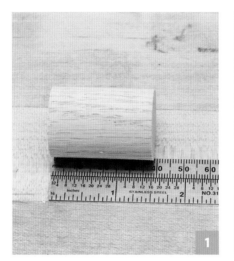

3 **Mark the dowel.** With a 1⅛ in.-wide piece of scrap as a guide, mark two parallel lines on one end of section 2.

4 **Refine the command module.** Clamp the 1½ in. dowel in a vise and flatten one side with a hand plane, adjusting as you go to create as flat a face as possible, until you reach the marked line and the width of the flattened face is at about 1 in. Turn the piece over and do the same on the other side to create two opposing flat faces. Set the piece aside.

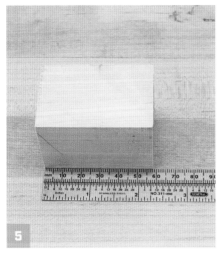

5 Now for the central unit—section 3. Mill a piece of stock to 1½ x 1½ and cut a 2¼ in. length.

6 Mark for an octagon. Guiding your pencil with a straight edge, mark a pencil line ½ in. in from both directions on all four sides. You should have eight pencil lines total.

7 Pick up your block plane. Plane the edges to the marked lines, creating four new faces. Repeat on all four corners to end up with an octagon with roughly equal width faces.

8 Mark for the bevels. Mark a pencil line ⅛ in. from each end on all eight faces of the piece, and again ⅛ in. from the faces on both ends.

BUILD THE MODULES *(continued)*

9 **Back to the block plane.** Bevel to the lines on both ends of the piece.

10 **Build the solar panels.** At the tablesaw, cut four 1½ x 4½ in. pieces of ¼ in. plywood.

11 **Plane the edges.** Plane the edges at approximately 30° on both faces along the two long sides and one short side. You're looking for a roughly ⅛ in.-wide bevel that exposes the interior of the plywood. Set the panels aside.

12 **Rout dadoes for the solar panels.** Set up your router at the router table with a ⅛ in. bit, with the fence in place to rout a centered dado on the face of section 3. Mark your stops on the fence (see Zangool Scout Fighter, page 72) and rout a 1½ in.-long stopped dado on all four faces. Adjust the fence as necessary to widen the dado until the panels fit it (¼ in. plywood is rarely true to size, which is why we're using a ⅛ in. bit and making the adjustments).

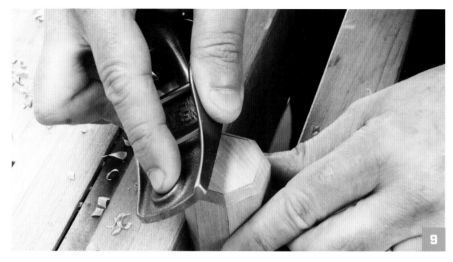

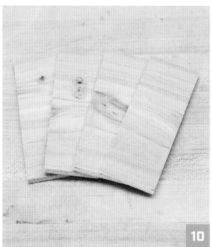

13 Build the orbital workshop—section 4. Cut off a 2 in. length of 1¼ in. dowel and set it aside for later use.

14 Mark for drilling. With a centering square, mark the center points on both ends of sections 1, 2, and 3, and on one end of section 4.

15 Head to the drill press. Insert a ½ in. brad-point bit and drill ⅜ in. deep holes into the center points as marked.

16 Add detail to the command module. With the same bit in place, drill two very shallow (1/32 in.) marks on both flat faces of section 2, centered ⅜ in. from each end of the piece. You're not drilling holes here, just scoring the surface with a pattern of two concentric circles (the interior one is a shallow hole created by the point of the drill).

BUILD THE MODULES *(continued)*

17 Drill for the antennae. Change out the bit to a ³/₁₆ in. brad-point bit and drill ¼ in.-deep holes on both faces of section 2, centered between the ½ in. drill marks created in step 15.

18 Drill for the base/hand-hold. Change out the bit again, now to a ³/₈ in. brad-point, and drill a centered ³/₈ in.-deep hole on one of the non-routed faces of section 3.

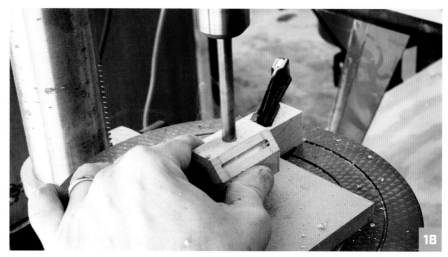

19 Time to sand. Lay down a sheet of 240-grit sandpaper on a flat surface and sand all the ends and faces of each section. Lightly round the edges, including those at the ends of the dowel sections.

FINISH THE BUILD

20 **Cut some more dowels.** You'll need one ½ in. length of ½ in. dowel, two ⅞ in. pieces of ½ in. dowel, one ⅝ in. piece of ½ in. dowel, and two 4¼ in. pieces of ³⁄₁₆ in. dowel.

21 **Insert the solar panels.** Brush a thin line of wood glue into each of the dadoes of the central unit and insert the non-beveled ends of the solar panels. The joint should fit tightly enough to hold without clamps. Check that the panels are square to each other, and set aside to dry, balanced on one end of the unit, for at least an hour.

22 **Link the sections.** Working on one section at a time, dab wood glue into the holes and connect the sections 1 through 3 with the two ⅞ in. pieces of ½ in. dowel. Connect section 3 to section 4 with the ½ in. length of ½ in. dowel.

23 **Add the outside module.** Dab wood glue into the remaining hole and insert the ⅝ in. piece of ½ in. dowel.

24 **Add the antennae.** Dot wood glue into the two 3/16 in. holes on the command module and insert the two pieces of 3/16 in. dowel.

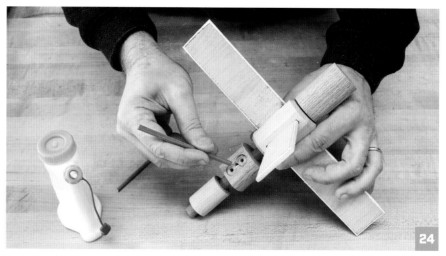

— CA-GLUE CLAMPING TRICK —

For standard glue-ups I turn to wood glue, spreading it on evenly but not too thickly because the joints won't see much stress. Use this clamping trick for the many small or oddly shaped pieces that it would be tough to clamp properly. (Generally I avoid using cyanoacrylate alone, since it doesn't create a very lasting bond.) Spread a generous but not excessive amount of wood glue on each gluing face, followed by no more than two or three dots of cyanoacrylate. I prefer the gel or "thick" cyanoacrylate, which won't soak into the wood and sets more quickly. Note that instead of using the stuff sold in the small tubes as "super glue," look for cyanoacrylate, which is available in larger bottles in a variety of viscosities. Press the piece firmly in place for about thirty seconds until the glue takes hold. Wait another few minutes, then wipe away squeeze-out with a damp rag or brush it away, getting into edges and corners with a lightly moistened old toothbrush.

25 **Apply finish.**
Pictured is three coats of spray lacquer, lightly sanded with 320 grit between coats—a classic and very fine finish.

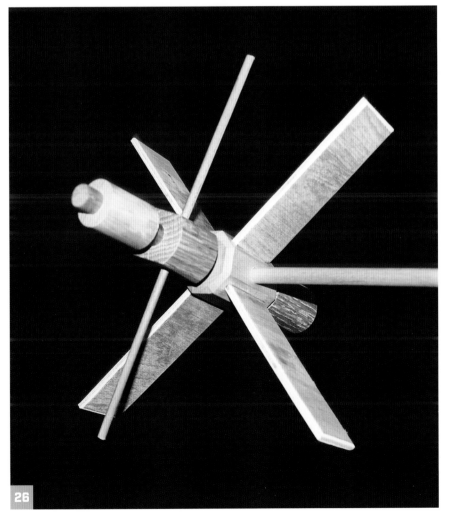

26 **Transmit data.**
Move the Sky Station slowly through the air, accompanied by softly echoing beeps, gurgling bits of speech, and static.

— 7 —
YBURIAN TRANSPORT

A couple of visits to the router table are essential to this build. The routed dadoes in the fuselage of the Yburian Transport create a strong joint for the large wings and fin, and using a cove bit to rout grooves into the outer wings ensures that the winglets are fully integrated. As with the Ice Fighter, laminating a darker wood between two layers of light-colored wood adds sleek detail, and you'll see yet another way to create a cockpit.

WHAT YOU'LL NEED

- Tablesaw
- Drill press or handheld drill
- Bench sander or orbital sander
- Bandsaw
- Square
- Block plane
- Pencil
- Spray adhesive
- Wood glue
- Gel cyanoacrylate
- Scissors
- Sandpaper (180, 240, 320 grits)
- Finish or paint(s) of your choice
- $\frac{1}{2}$ in. Forstner or brad-point drill bit
- $\frac{3}{8}$ in. brad-point drill bit
- Router and router table
- $\frac{3}{8}$ in. router straight bit
- $\frac{1}{2}$ in. router cove bit
- $\frac{1}{8}$ in. router straight bit
- $\frac{1}{8}$ in. wood chisel
- 3–4 small bar clamps
- Scrap wood cauls
- Centering square
- 1 copy of template 1
- 3 copies of template 2
- 2 copies of template 3

MATERIALS

QTY	PART	DIMENSIONS
1	Fuselage	$\frac{11}{16}$ x $\frac{7}{8}$ x 5 in.
1	Cockpit dowel (contrasting stock)	$\frac{1}{2}$ x $\frac{1}{2}$ in.
2	Wings/fin	$\frac{1}{8}$ x $4\frac{3}{8}$ x 13 in.
1	Wings/fin (contrasting stock)	$\frac{1}{8}$ x $4\frac{3}{8}$ x 13 in.
2	Winglet dowels (contrasting stock)	$4\frac{3}{4}$ x $\frac{1}{2}$ in.
2	Gun dowels	2 x $\frac{3}{16}$ in.
1	Small fins (contrasting stock)	1 x $5\frac{1}{2}$ x $\frac{1}{8}$ in.
2	Engine dowels (contrasting stock)	2 x $\frac{5}{8}$ in.
2	Engine dowels (contrasting stock)	1 x $\frac{1}{2}$ in.

TEMPLATES: YBURIAN TRANSPORT

Copy at 100%

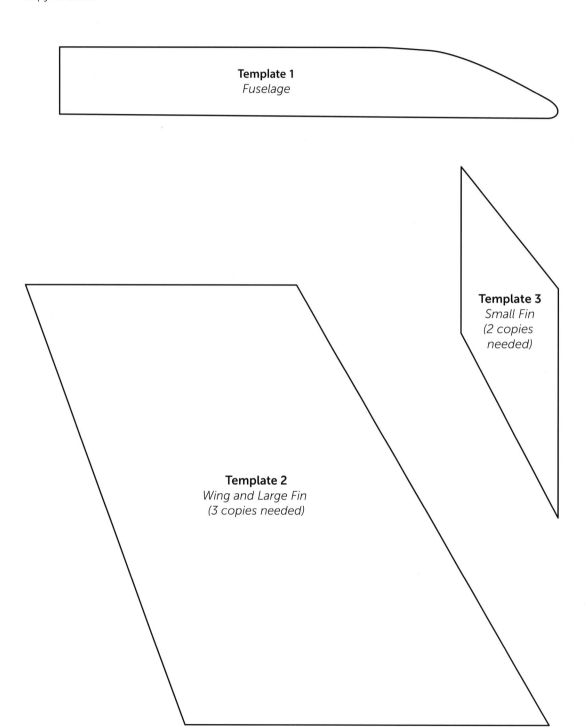

Template 1
Fuselage

Template 3
*Small Fin
(2 copies
needed)*

Template 2
*Wing and Large Fin
(3 copies needed)*

THE FUSELAGE

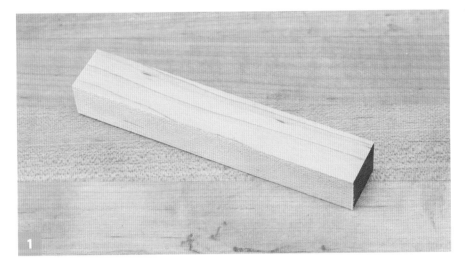

1 Source the material. Start things off with an ¹¹⁄₁₆ x ⅞ x 5 in. piece of stock milled from a worthy piece dug out of the scrap bin.

2 Drill for the cockpit. At the drill press, drill a ½ in. hole ⅜ in. deep into the ⅞ in. face of the stock, centered ½ in. from one end.

3 Insert the cockpit. Dab some wood glue into the hole and insert a ½ in. length of ½ in. dowel. Use a contrasting wood to that of the fuselage so the cockpit really pops.

THE FUSELAGE *(continued)*

4 **Cut it out.** Spray adhesive onto template 1 and apply it to the ¾ in. face of the stock, with the rounded tip facing the end in which you inserted the cockpit. Cut to the lines at the bandsaw without going over.

5 **Smooth it.** At the bench sander, sand to the lines and smooth the piece, rounding the nose and removing bandsaw blade marks and the template.

6 **Drill for the base/ hand-hold.** Drill a ⅜ in. hole centered on the underside of the fuselage, ⅜ in. deep. Position it about 1½ in. from the tail-end of the piece since the finished ship will be heavily weighted toward the tail.

7 **Mark for routing.** With the help of a square, draw a line on all four sides of the piece, 3⅝ in. from the back end.

8 **Rout for the wings.** Set up your router at the router table with a ⅜ in. bit set ⅛ in. above the surface of the table, and with the fence ⅛ in. from the bit. Mark the outer edges of the bit on your temporary fence and rout along the two sides, always referencing the top face of the piece against the fence.

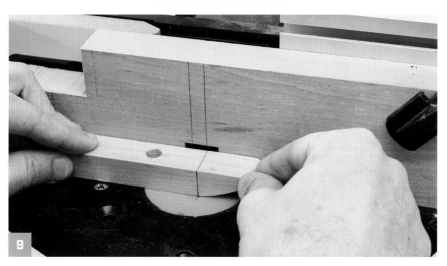

9 **Rout for the main fin.** Adjust the fence so the bit is ¼ in. from the fence and rout along the top of the piece.

THE FUSELAGE *(continued)*

10 **Grab a chisel.** Square up the ends of the routed dadoes.

11 **Fine-tune it.** With a plane and/or 240-grit sandpaper, smooth the edges and nose to your satisfaction.

THE WINGS/FIN

12 **Source the materials.** You'll need two 4⅜ x 13 in. pieces of ⅛ in. stock and one 4⅜ x 13 in. piece of contrasting ⅛ in. stock.

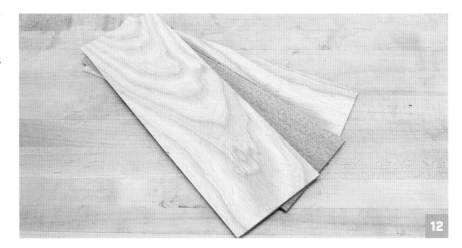

13 **Glue it up.** Spread wood glue on one side of each of the two like pieces and sandwich the contrasting piece between. Clamp together, using additional boards and scrap wood as cauls to keep the boards aligned with even pressure to prevent warping. Set aside to dry for at least two hours.

14 **Trim it.** At the jointer and tablesaw, even up the edges as necessary, trimming the board down to 4¼ x 12½ in.

15 **Apply the wing and large fin templates.** Make three copies of template 2, spray with adhesive, and apply them to the board, arranging them as shown.

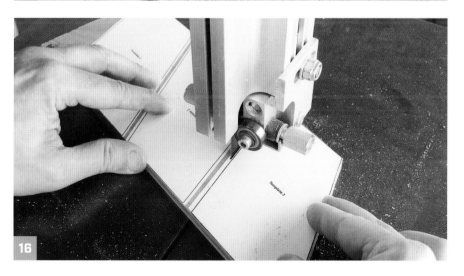

16 **Cut them out.** At the bandsaw, cut to the lines without going over.

THE WINGS/FINS [continued]

17 **Smoothing time.** Head to the bench sander and sand with 240 grit to remove the bandsaw marks. Lightly round the front outside corner of each piece. Remove the templates with an orbital sander, using 240 grit.

18 **Rout for the winglets.** Set up your router at the router table with a ½ in. cove bit and set the fence ¼ in. from the center of the bit. Run the outer edges of two of the pieces over the bit, proceeding slowly and bracing them firmly against the fence. These are the wings.

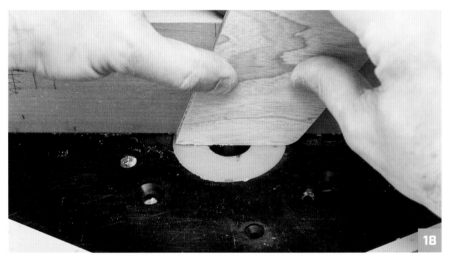

19 **Rout for the small fins.** Swap out the cove bit for a ⅛ in. straight bit, setting it to protrude ⅛ in. above the tabletop. Set the fence ½ in. from the bit. Run the top edge of the large fin (the remaining piece you didn't rout with the cove bit) along the fence on both sides, routing shallow 2⅛ in. long stopped dadoes. Square the ends of both dadoes using a ⅛ in. chisel.

20 **Fine-tune the wings and large fin.** With a block plane, create ⅛ in.-wide 45° chamfers along the leading edges of the wings and large fin, plus the top edge of the large fin.

21 **Cut dowels for the winglets.** You need two 4¾ in. lengths of ½ in. dowel and two 2 in. lengths of ³⁄₁₆ in. dowel.

22 **Drill for the guns.** Mark the centers on one end of each of the winglet dowels and drill ³⁄₁₆ in. holes ¼ in. deep. Clamp together two scrap blocks to create a corner in which you can stabilize the pieces and ensure you drill straight holes.

23 **Add the guns.** Glue the 2 in. long ³/₁₆ in. dowels into the holes.

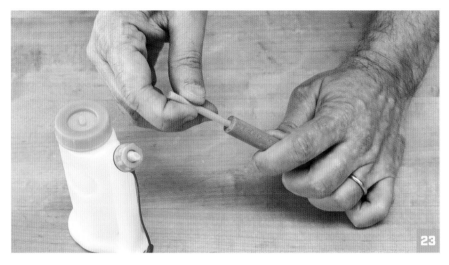

24 **Attach the winglets.** Check that the dowels fit fully into the coved outer edges. If not, lightly sand the cove with a piece of 240-grit sandpaper wrapped around a dowel. Dot the coved outer edge of each wing with wood glue and gel cyanoacrylate and attach the dowels, with the front edges of the ½ in. dowels aligned with the front edges of the routed coves. Press and hold firmly in place for at least thirty seconds. Set aside.

25 **Apply the small fin templates.** Glue two copies of template 3 to a 1 x 5½ in. piece of ⅛ in. stock, lining them up at the edge of the stock so the grain runs parallel to the interior edge of the fin.

26 **Cut out the small fins.** At the bandsaw, cut to the lines without going over.

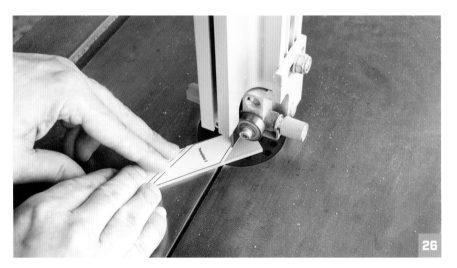

27 Fine-tune the fins. At the bench sander, sand to the template lines and lightly square off the pointed tips. Remove the templates with an orbital sander or by hand-sanding.

28 Attach the small fins. Wood glue the small fins into the dadoes as shown.

— WORKING WITH SMALL PARTS —

In a book filled with projects that include many small parts, I can't neglect to add a reminder that working safely, whether on Earth or in outer space, is Rule #1. Whenever possible, try to cut small pieces from a larger piece of stock that you can comfortably support while keeping your fingers away from moving blades. Hold a small piece in a clamp to maneuver it at the bench sander or bandsaw. Advance pieces slowly to keep them from flying into space (save that for your finished ships) and use push sticks, grip paddles, or the eraser tip of a long pencil to hold down the pieces.

THE ENGINES

29 **Cut some dowels.** At the tablesaw, cut two 2 in. lengths of ⅝ in. dowel and two 1 in. lengths of ½ in. dowel.

30 **Mark the centers.** With your centering square, mark the centers of both ends of each ⅝ in. dowel.

31 **Step over to the drill press.** Set it up with a ½ in. brad-point bit. Drill ⅛ in.-deep holes into one end of each of the ⅝ in. dowels. Drill a very shallow (no more than 1/32 in.) mark into the opposite ends (simulating the intakes of the engines, just as we did with the Quasar Fighter).

32 **Glue time.** Spread some wood glue into the holes and insert the ½ in. dowels. Set the completed engines aside.

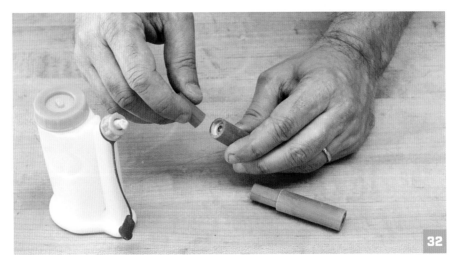

THE FINAL BUILD

33 **Attach the wings and large fin.** One at a time, spread a thin line of wood glue into each routed dado and insert pieces. The fit should be tight enough to hold them in place.

34 **Attach the engines.** Working with one engine at a time, spread a thin line of gel cyanoacrylate along the wing and edge of the fuselage, and attach the engine so the rear edge of the $\frac{5}{8}$ in. dowel aligns with the back end of the fuselage. Hold in place for at least thirty seconds.

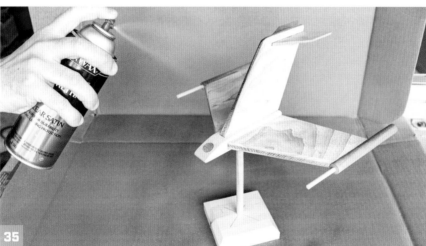

35 **Finish it.** Apply your favorite finish. Shown here is three coats of spray polyurethane, sanded lightly with 320 grit between each coat.

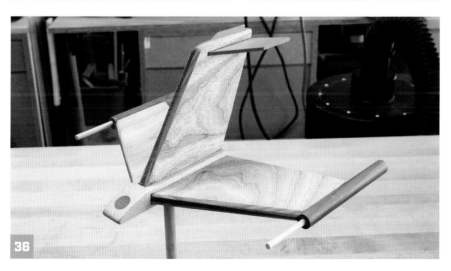

36 **Transport.** Cruise at sub-light speed through intergalactic space, transporting valuable minerals, cyber-soldiers, and power cells between distant planets.

— 8 —

BATTLESHIP POLUMETIS

Time for the big one. When designing the Polumetis, I envisioned a ship of such massive size that most if not all the other ships in this book would look tiny next to it, and in fact would be able to dock at one of its many bays. While this one's not quite to the true scale I imagined, I think it reaches nicely for that awe-inspiring grandeur. You are, of course, at liberty to go for it and build this to the appropriate dimensions relative to the other ships in this book. I figure a couple of 4 x 8 ft. sheets of quality 3/4 in. plywood would give you just enough material to work with!

WHAT YOU'LL NEED

- Tablesaw
- Drill press or handheld drill
- Bench sander or orbital sander
- Bandsaw
- Square
- Block plane
- Pencil
- Spray adhesive
- Wood glue
- Gel cyanoacrylate
- Scissors
- Sandpaper (180, 240, 320 grits)
- Finish or paint(s) of your choice
- $3/8$ in. brad-point drill bit
- $3/16$ in. brad-point drill bit
- $3/4$ in. Forstner drill bit
- 1–2 small bar clamps
- 1 copy each of templates 1, 3, 4, and 5
- 2 copies of template 2

MATERIALS

QTY	PART	DIMENSIONS
1	Hull	$1/2$ x 5 x 12 in.
1	Hull	$1/4$ x 5 x 25 in.
9	Gun dowels	$3/16$ x $3/16$ in.
1	Bridge tower	$1/4$ x 1 x 4 in.
1	Bridge tower dowel	$5/8$ x $3/16$ in.
1	Drilling jig	1 x $1\frac{1}{8}$ x $1\frac{1}{8}$ in.
1	Engine dowel	1 x 1 in.
1	Connector dowel	$11/16$ x $3/4$ in.

TEMPLATES: BATTLESHIP POLUMETIS

Copy at 100%

Notes:
Five templates in one.
Cut and piece together on dotted lines.

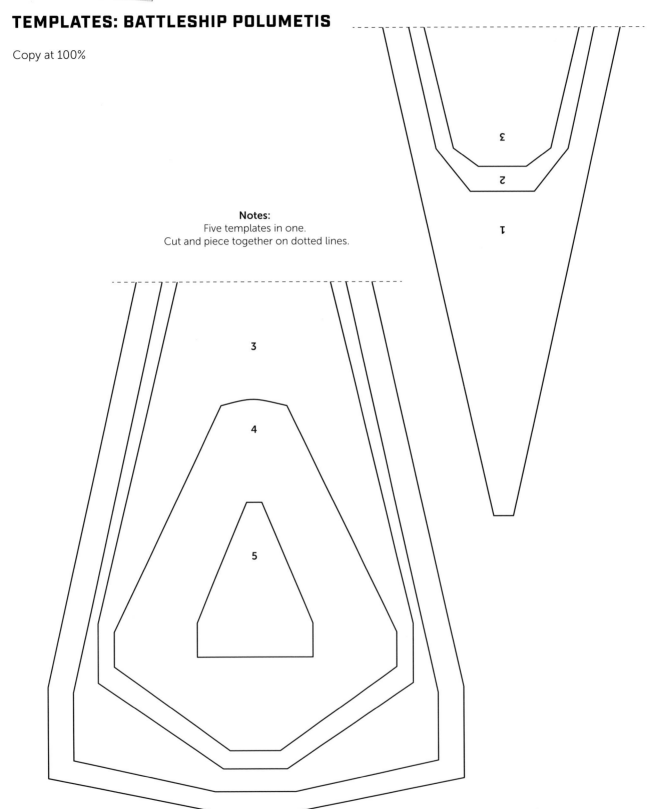

THE HULL

1 Prepare the templates. Note that the templates as provided are layered pretty much as they'll be in the finished piece. Print and cut out one copy each of templates 1, 3, 4, and 5, and two copies of template 2.

2 Apply the templates. Spray adhesive on template 1 (the largest) and apply it to a 5 x 12 in. piece of ½ in. stock (the finished ship will be painted, so scrap MDF works). Spray adhesive on each of the other templates one at a time, and apply them to a 5 x 25 in. piece of ¼ in. stock, arranging as shown to minimize waste.

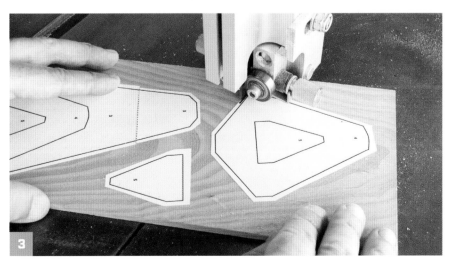

3 Head to the bandsaw. Cut out the pieces, cutting close to the templates lines without going over.

4 Sand to the lines. At the bench sander, sand to the template lines and smooth the edges of all the pieces.

5 Bevel the edges. With a block plane, create a 45° ⅛ in. chamfer along the front edges of section 1, a ¹⁄₁₆ in. chamfer along the front edges of section 2, and a ¹⁄₁₆ in. chamfer along all the edges of sections 3, 4, and 5. Chamfer the main hull top and bottom, and all other pieces just on one side.

6 Give it another sanding. With an orbital sander or by hand, sand all the pieces to 320 grit, removing the templates in the process. Avoid rounding over the chamfered edges.

7 Glue up the large sections. Apply wood glue and a few dots of gel cyanoacrylate to one of the two section 2 pieces and hold it to the top of the main hull for thirty seconds, centered across the width and ⅛ in. from the rear of the main hull as shown. Do the same with the second section 2, attaching it to the bottom of the main hull.

8 Clamp it. Allow the cyanoacrylate gel to set and clamp the pieces between two boards (I used some scrap plywood). Set aside to dry completely.

9 Stack the other sections. Working on one section at a time, apply wood glue and a few dots of gel cyanoacrylate to sections 3, 4, and 5, stacking and positioning them as shown.

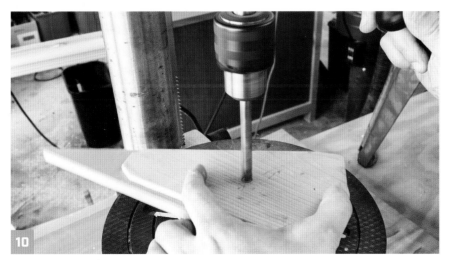

10 Drill for the base/ hand-hold. Drill a ⅜ in. hole centered on the underside of the hull, ⅜ in. deep.

THE GUN TURRETS

11 **Head to the drill press.** Drill ⅛ in.-deep ³⁄₁₆ in. holes into nine spots, three each on sections 1, 3, and 4. Exact placement is not important here, but try to spread them out randomly and focus on strategic positions that will protect the ship from enemy fighters on all sides.

12 **Add the dowels.** Dab the holes with wood glue and tap in ³⁄₁₆ in. lengths of ³⁄₁₆ in. dowel.

THE BRIDGE TOWER

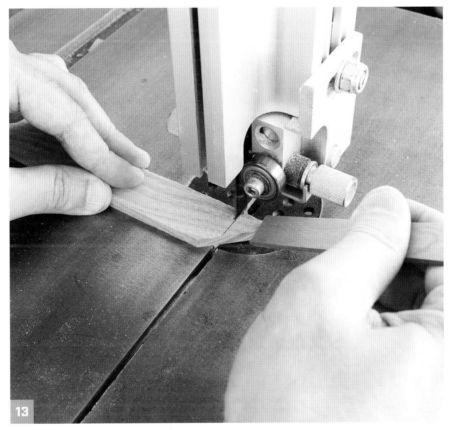

13 **Make a bridge.** At the bandsaw or tablesaw, cut a triangular piece of stock off one corner of a ¼ in. board, so that each side of the triangle measures ¾ in. Use a piece of scrap to push the piece and keep your fingers far from the blade. Sand the piece smooth at the bench sander or by hand.

14 **Drill a hole.** At the drill press, drill a ³/₁₆ in. hole ⅛ in. deep into the center of the piece.

15 **Build the tower.** Glue a ⅝ in. length of ³/₁₆ in. dowel into the hole. Set the piece aside.

THE ENGINE

16 **Make a drilling jig.** Mill a square 1 x 1⅛ x 1⅛ in. piece of stock. At the drill press, drill a centered ¾ in. hole through it with a Forstner bit, gripping the stock to ensure a straight hole. Proceed slowly and back out frequently to clear the shavings. Set the jig aside.

17 **Build the engine.** At the drill press with the ¾ in. Forstner bit in place, drill a centered ¼ in.-deep hole into one end of a 1 in. length of 1 in. dowel. Drill a scant 1/32 in.-deep mark into the opposite end.

18 **Drill into the fuselage.** Position the fuselage tail-end up in a vise. Firmly hold or clamp the jig centered onto the back end. With the ¾ in. Forstner bit in a hand-held drill, drill through the jig ½ in. deep.

19 Attach the engine. Use wood glue to attach an $^{11}/_{16}$ in. length of $^3/_4$ in. dowel into the hole in the fuselage. Apply wood glue into the $^1/_4$ in. deep hole in the 1 in. dowel and attach it to the protruding end of the connecting dowel. It should be flush to the fuselage. Set the piece aside to dry.

THE FINAL BUILD

20 Drill for the tower. At the drill press, drill a $^3/_{16}$ in. hole $^3/_{16}$ in. deep, centered into the top platform.

THE FINAL BUILD (continued)

21 **Attach the tower.** Dab wood glue into the ³/₁₆ in. hole and insert the tower (unless you prefer to paint it, then wait until the next step).

22 **Paint it.** You can apply your favorite finish, or for some imperial shine spray on two coats of gray primer followed by three coats of metallic silver. Spray the tower with metallic dark grey before gluing it on and add small details in acrylic red paint to the front tip and the engine exhaust.

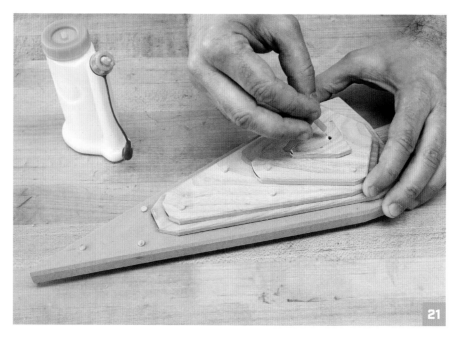

— FINISHING YOUR SHIPS —

When it comes to finish, my usual choice is Danish oil. It's easy to apply, very forgiving, and brings out the wood grain beautifully. But you have many options, and I encourage you to try several, as I've done with the projects in this book. For a glossy back-to-nature finish you can grate beeswax into mineral oil (3 parts oil to 2 parts wax) and melt it gently over low heat. Let it cool, apply with a rag, and buff to a shine. Spray lacquer or spray polyurethane provide an easy durable finish and a more "pro" look, and the spray makes it easier to get the finish into all the corners of some of the more complicated ships. I like three coats of satin, lightly sanding with 320 grit between coats. Of course, you may also choose to paint your finished fighter, either in traditional battle silvers and greys or in some sleek reds and yellows. The other side of the universe, as they say in outer space, is the limit.

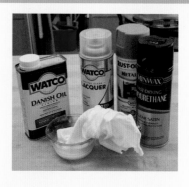

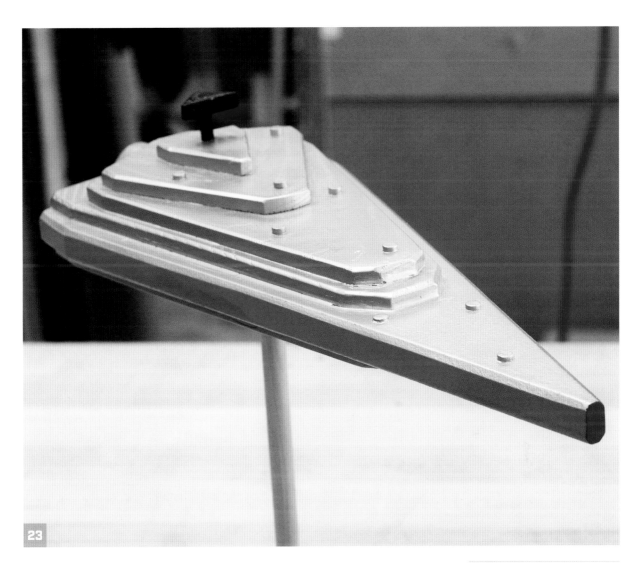

23 **Cruise ominously.** Set the scene with the menacing music of your choice. Hoist the battleship and move it ever-so-slowly. Make creaking and grumbling noises as the massive ship dominates intergalactic space.

— 9 —

THE CENTURION SCORPION

This project takes things to a new level by employing a broad catalog of techniques: bandsawing a curved template, drilling multiple holes for dowels, routing a mortise, and chamfering an octagon. The appearance is also of a different order: familiar, yet menacing and alien, while clearly reminiscent of its namesake arachnid. Don't tell the other projects, but if I had to choose a favorite, this one could be it.

WHAT YOU'LL NEED

- Tablesaw
- Drill press or handheld drill
- Bench sander or orbital sander
- Bandsaw
- Square
- Block plane
- Pencil
- Spray adhesive
- Wood glue
- Gel cyanoacrylate
- Scissors
- Sandpaper (180, 240, 320 grits)
- Finish or paint(s) of your choice
- Router and router table
- $\frac{1}{4}$ in. router straight bit
- $\frac{1}{4}$ in. wood chisel
- $\frac{3}{8}$ in. brad-point drill bit
- $\frac{3}{16}$ in. brad-point drill bit
- $\frac{3}{16}$ in. skip-tooth bandsaw blade
- 2 copies of template 1
- 1 copy of template 2

MATERIALS

QTY	PART	DIMENSIONS
1	Fuselage	$1\frac{5}{8}$ x $1\frac{5}{8}$ x 4 in.
2	Wing connectors	$\frac{1}{4}$ x $1\frac{3}{16}$ x 3 in.
1	Wing angles	$\frac{13}{16}$ x 3 x 4 in.
1	Wing	$\frac{1}{2}$ x 4 x 8 in.
2	Main guns	$\frac{5}{16}$ x $\frac{5}{16}$ x $1\frac{1}{4}$ in.
2	Main gun barrels	4 x $\frac{3}{16}$ in.
1	Tail	$\frac{1}{2}$ x $2\frac{1}{4}$ x $4\frac{3}{4}$ in.
1	Tail gun dowel	$\frac{3}{8}$ x $1\frac{1}{8}$ in.
1	Tail gun dowel	$\frac{3}{16}$ X 3 in.
1	Tail connector dowel	$\frac{3}{8}$ x $\frac{3}{16}$ in.

TEMPLATES:
THE CENTURION SCORPION

Copy at 100%

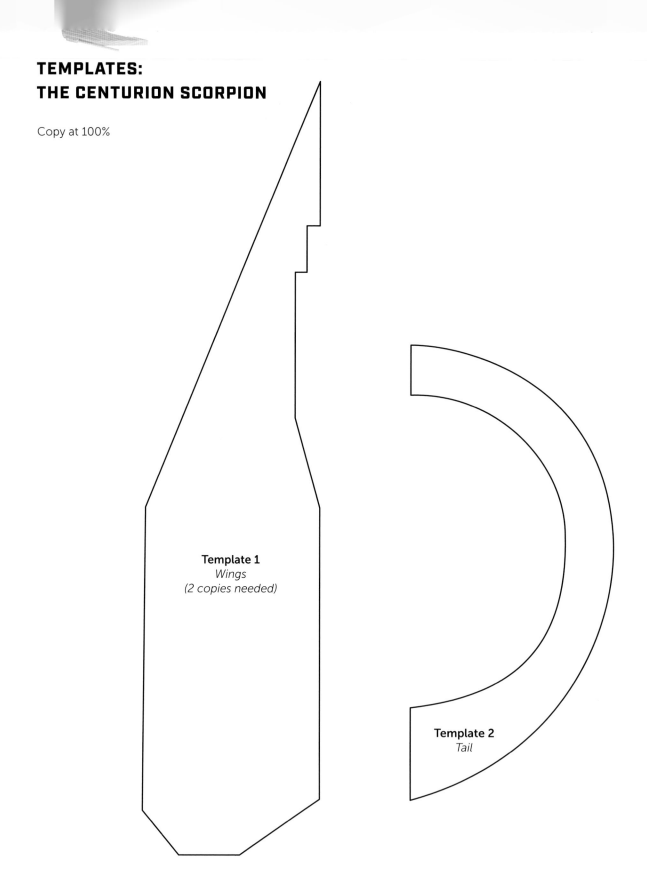

Template 1
Wings
(2 copies needed)

Template 2
Tail

THE FUSELAGE

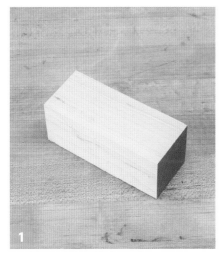

1 **Source your stock.**
You'll need a 1⅝ x 1⅝ x 4 in. piece of stock in the wood of your choice, like this scrap maple.

2 **Mark for the tenons.**
Make a pencil mark ½ in. from each end of the stock, on two opposing faces.

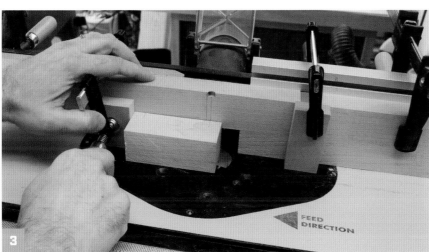

3 **Set up the router.**
Insert a ¼ in. straight-edged bit into your router and install it in your router table. Lining up the pencil marks on the stock with the outer edges of the bit, position two stop blocks as shown so you can rout a 3 in. stopped dado, leaving ½ in. at each end of the stock. Position the fence for a centered dado, ⅝ in. from the cutting edge of the bit.

FEED DIRECTION

4 **Rout the tenons.**
Make a few passes, raising the bit until you reach a depth of ³⁄₁₆ in., to rout the tenons on two opposing sides of the piece. Make sure you reference the same face against the fence as you rout each side. Leave the router set-up in place; you'll use it again in a little while.

THE FUSELAGE [continued]

5 **Square the ends of the tenons.** With a sharp ¼ in. chisel, square off each end of the tenon.

6 **Drill for the tail.** Mark the center on one end of the piece and drill a ¼ in.-deep, ⅜ in. hole.

7 **Drill for the base/hand-hold.** With the same bit in place, drill a ⅜ in. hole centered on the underside of the fuselage (one of the two sides at a right angle to the routed sides), ⅜ in. deep.

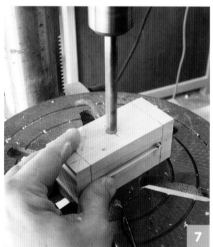

8 **Mark for the octagon.** Using a square as a guide, mark a pencil line ⁷⁄₁₆ in. from all four edges, on all four faces of the piece.

9 **Turn it into an octagon.** Either at the tablesaw with the blade at 45° or with a hand plane (the safer option), chamfer all four edges to the lines so you have an eight-sided piece.

10 **Chamfer the ends.** Set your tablesaw blade to 45°. Brace the piece against your miter gauge and adjust its position so the top edge of the angled blade comes in ¼ in. from the end of the piece. Chamfer the edges along all faces of the piece to create an octagonal dome. Repeat with the other end of the piece.

11 **Time to sand.** Lay a sheet of 240-grit sandpaper on a flat surface and sand each side and each chamfered corner smooth.

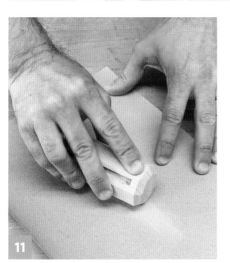

12 **Attach the wing connectors.** Mill two 1³⁄₁₆ x 3 in. pieces of ¼ in. stock and attach with wood glue into the tenons on each side of the main pod, using your square to ensure they're at perfect right angles to the fuselage.

THE FUSELAGE *(continued)*

13 Cut the angled strips. With the tablesaw blade set at 10°, cut four 3 in. strips from a piece of $1\frac{3}{16}$ in. stock. The strips should be $\frac{3}{16}$ in. thick at the thickest edge.

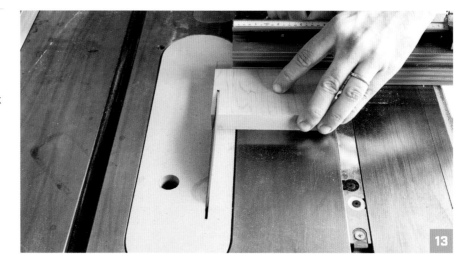

14 Accessorize your look. Glue the strips onto the wing connections with the thickest edge against the fuselage.

THE WINGS

15 Apply the templates. Glue two copies of template 1 onto a 4 x 8 in. piece of $\frac{1}{2}$ in. stock.

16 Cut out the wings. At the bandsaw, cut to the lines without going over. Take extra care to ensure the interior stepped pattern is square and to the line.

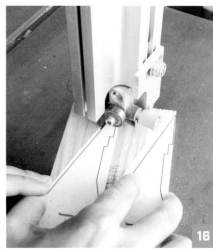

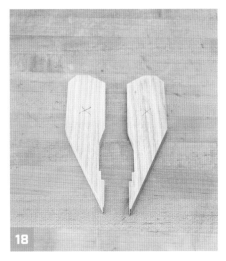

17 **Refine the wings.** At the bench sander or with an orbital sander, remove the templates and the bandsaw blade marks and smooth the piece.

18 **Mark the wings.** Set the wings down in what will be their final position. Mark the two visible sides in pencil with an X.

19 **Rout the dadoes.** Return to the router and set the fence ⅛ in. from the ¼ in. bit you left in place back at step 4. Make a few passes, raising the bit until you reach a depth of ³⁄₁₆ in., to rout the dadoes along the back interior edge of each wing as shown, keeping the sides marked with an X against the fence.

20 **Chamfer the edges.** With a block plane, create a 45°, ¹⁄₁₆ in.-wide chamfer around the exterior edges of the wings on both sides.

THE GUNS

21 **Mill your stock.** You'll need two 1¼ in. lengths of ⁵⁄₁₆ x ⁵⁄₁₆ in. stock.

22 **Drill.** On each piece, mark the center on one end. At the drill press, drill a centered ³⁄₁₆ in. hole ¼ in. deep.

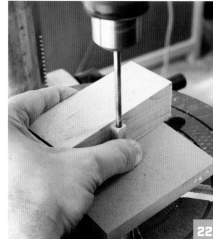

23 **Refine.** At the bench sander, soften the edges along one aside of each piece and create rounded chamfers at both ends of each piece.

24 **Attach the barrels.** Glue two 4 in. lengths of ³⁄₁₆ in. dowel into the holes. Set the pieces aside.

THE TAIL

25 **Apply the template.** Spray a copy of template 2 with adhesive and attach to a 2¼ x 4¾ in. piece of ½ in. stock, lining it up so the two ends of the image meet the edge of the stock. Make sure the grain runs along the 4¾ in. length of the stock.

26 **Drill holes.** Mark centered holes into the side of the stock at both ends of the templated image and drill ⅜ in. holes ⅛ in. deep.

27 **Set up the bandsaw.** For best results with the tight curve in this piece, use a ³⁄₁₆ in. skip-tooth blade with four teeth per inch.

THE TAIL *(continued)*

28 **Cut out the tail.** Cut along the template lines, sticking close to it without going over.

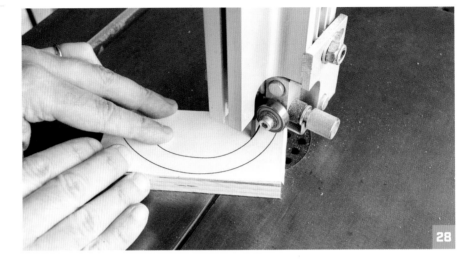

29 **Fine-tune the tail.** At the bench sander, sand to the lines, removing the bandsaw marks and the templates, and round out the piece for a more tubular shape that narrows near the gun barrel. Finish the rounding by hand with 240 grit.

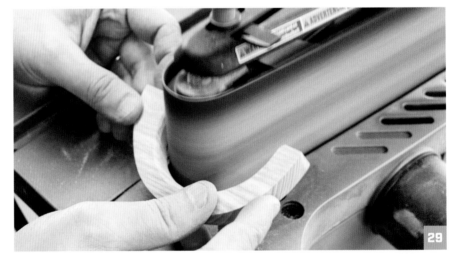

30 **Mill the gun barrels.** You'll need a 1⅛ in. piece of ⅜ in. dowel and a 3 in. piece of ³⁄₁₆ in. dowel.

31 **Drill it out.** Mark the center of one end of the ⅜ in. dowel. At the drill press, drill a ³⁄₁₆ in. hole ⅛ in. deep.

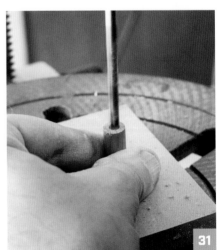

32 **Glue up the tail.** Glue the 3/16 in. dowel into the 3/8 in. dowel, then glue this piece into the narrower end of the tail. Set the pieces aside.

THE FINAL BUILD

33 **Attach the guns to the wings.** Working on one wing at a time, use cyanoacrylate to glue the guns to the outer wing so they are 3/16 in. forward of the outer corner at the back of the wing. I marked a pencil line 3/16 in. from the end of a strip of 3/32 in.-thick scrap for an impromptu jig to help line things up.

THE FINAL BUILD *(continued)*

34 **Attach the tail.** Glue a ³⁄₁₆ in. length of ⅜ in. dowel into the open end of the tail piece, and then glue it into the back end of the fuselage, ensuring that the tail is centered over the fuselage as shown.

35 **Attach the wings.** Spread wood glue into the dados on the wings and fit them over the tenons on the fuselage. The fit should be tight enough to hold without clamps.

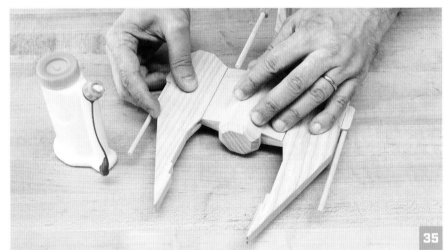

36 **Finish it.** Apply the finish of your choice. Pictured is three coats of spray lacquer, sanded lightly with 320 grit between coats.

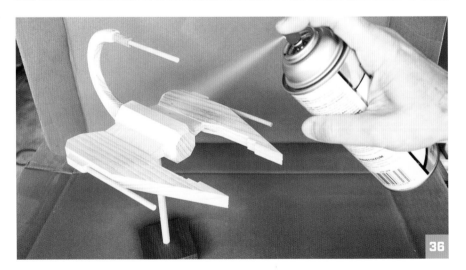

37

Create mayhem. Zero in on an enemy destroyer's command center with all three guns, but especially with that deadly scorpion tail.

— 10 —
GIZELDAN GUARDIAN

everal features make this one stand out: the double-pronged arrangement of the wings, further elongated by the guns; the exhaust system that foregoes external pipes; and the long central cockpit embedded into the fuselage. Throw in the prominent tiered winglets, and it all makes for an ultra-sleek and deadly spacecraft.

WHAT YOU'LL NEED

- Tablesaw
- Drill press or handheld drill
- Bench sander or orbital sander
- Bandsaw
- Square
- Block plane
- Pencil
- Spray adhesive
- Wood glue
- Gel cyanoacrylate
- Scissors
- Sandpaper (180, 240, 320 grits)

- Finish or paint(s) of your choice
- ½ in. Forstner or brad-point drill bit
- ⅜ in. brad-point drill bit
- 1–2 small bar clamps or a bench vise
- Router and router table
- ½ in. router cove bit
- 2 copies each of templates 1 and 2

MATERIALS

QTY	PART	DIMENSIONS
1	Pod	¾ x 2¼ x 4 in.
1	Cockpit dowel (contrasting stock)	4 x ½ in.
1	Wings	¼ x 4½ x 7½ in.
1	Wing details (contrasting stock)	¾ x 3 x 4¼ in.
2	Gun dowels	7 x ⅛ in.

TEMPLATES: GIZELDAN GUARDIAN

Copy at 100%

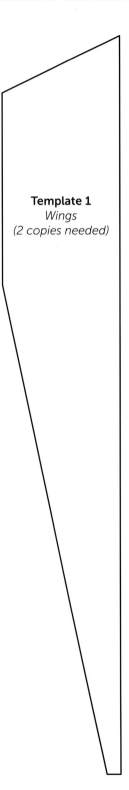

Template 1
*Wings
(2 copies needed)*

Template 2
*Small Wings
(2 copies needed)*

THE POD

1 Source the stock. You'll need a 4 x 2¼ in. piece of ¾ in. stock for the main body, in a wood color that will contrast with the dowel of the cockpit, such as maple, to go with a cherry dowel.

2 Drill the exhaust chambers. At the drill press, drill two ½ in. holes ⅝ in. deep into one end of the piece. They should be centered along the horizontal ¾ in. thickness and positioned 9/16 in. from each side.

3 Drill for the base/ hand-hold. Drill a ⅜ in. hole centered on the underside of the fuselage, ⅜ in. deep.

THE POD *(continued)*

4 **Fire up the router.** Set up a ½ in. cove bit in the router, adjusting the fence so it's ⅞ in. from the edge of the piece. Make a few passes, raising the bit each time, to rout a ¼ in.-deep groove into the top of the piece along the 4 in. length.

5 **Chamfer the sides.** Set up your tablesaw for a 30° cut and chamfer both long sides of the piece, running it against the fence.

6 **Insert the cockpit.** Cut a 4 in. length of ½ in. dowel in a contrasting stock and glue it into the routed groove. It'll likely be a tight fit, so you may need to squeeze it together in a vise or with clamps.

7 **Chamfer the back end.** With your tablesaw blade still set at 30°, use your miter gauge to chamfer the drilled end of the piece, creating an uplifted tail. Given the raised cockpit, you'll need to make the cut with the bottom side of the piece flat to the table. With a left-tilting tablesaw as shown, position the miter gauge in the slot to the right of the blade to get the angled cut in the correct direction.

8 **Chamfer the front end.** Adjust the blade angle to 45° and shift the miter gauge to the opposing slot to chamfer a "front hood" for the pod.

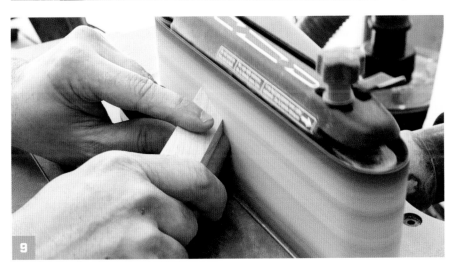

9 **Refine it.** At the bench sander or by hand, smooth the piece. Lightly round the front and back but do not round the side edges.

THE WINGS

10 **Prepare the stock.**
With your tablesaw blade set to 30°, chamfer the two long edges of a 4½ x 7½ in. piece of ¼ in. stock.

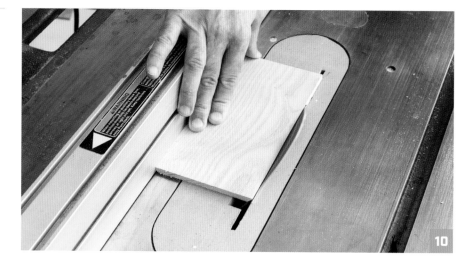

11 **Apply templates.**
Cut out two copies each of templates 1 and 2, with one template 1 cut to the lines. Position your stock with the newly cut chamfers face down and glue on the templates. Line up the larger templates as shown, so that the pointed tips and the longer edges meet the chamfered edges of the stock, and with the template you cut to the lines applied face down.

12 **Cut out the wing sections.** At the bandsaw, cut close to the lines/edges without going over.

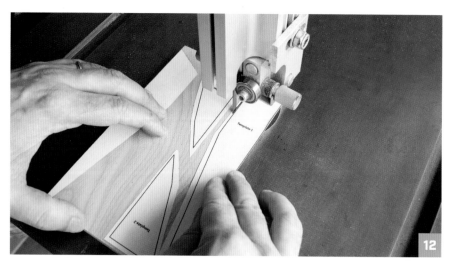

13 **Head to the bench sander.** Sand to the template lines/edges, removing the band saw blade marks. Sand away the templates.

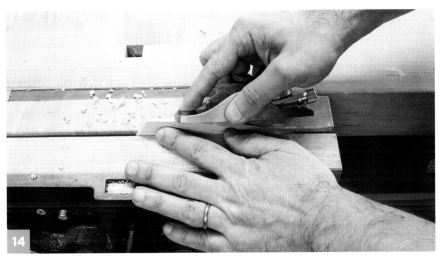

14 **Shape the wings.** With a block plane or at the bench sander, lightly round the top edges of the two smaller wing sections.

15 **Chamfer the edges.** With a block plane, chamfer the bottom edges of all four wing sections at 30°. Don't worry about being super-accurate; sighting by eye is fine.

THE WINGS *(continued)*

16 **Create detail.** Tilt your tablesaw blade to 45° and create a ⅛ in.-wide chamfer along the long edge of a 3 x 4 ¼ x ¾ in. piece of stock in the same species of wood you used for the cockpit. Move the fence over ⅝ in. and cut away the corner you just chamfered to create a thin shallow strip chamfered on two sides.

17 **Create detail, part two.** At the tablesaw, cut the strip into two 2 in. pieces. Using a miter gauge or sled, carefully chamfer both ends of each piece at 45°. You'll end up with two 2 in.-long shallow, flat-topped, pyramid-shaped pieces. The eraser tip of a pencil helps hold the small piece in place while keeping your fingers far from the blade.

18 **Add detail.** Glue the strips to the side of each wing, ¼ in. from the top edge and ⅞ in. from the back edge of wing, aligning the pieces with a square.

19 **Glue up the wings.** Glue the small wing sections to the bottom edges of the large wing sections as shown.

THE FINAL BUILD

20 **Attach the wings.** Glue the wings to the pod, aligning the chamfered top edges with the top edges of the fuselage sides.

21 **Attach the guns.** Cut two 7 in. lengths of ⅛ in. dowel and chamfer them at one end at 45°, either at the tablesaw or with a block plane. Glue to the interior edge of each wing, with the chamfered end of the dowel up against the angled hood of the fuselage.

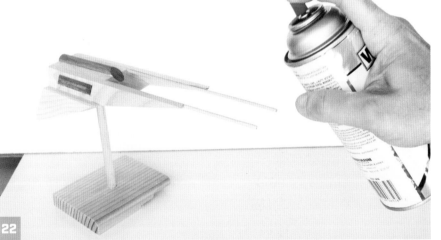

22 **Finish it.** Choose your favorite. Given this ship's many nooks and crannies, spray lacquer is a good choice.

23 **Land safely in alien territory.** Cruise this one slowly to a few inches above the surface of the planet (or workbench) and hover for a moment before settling into place. Double check atmospheric conditions before exiting the spacecraft.

ANELEAN STARBLADE

Take your time refining the fuselage and the gun chambers on the Starblade. With the wings essentially turned around from what we're used to seeing, the chamfers, sharp points, and keenly tapered nose help define the forward direction and create the distinctive look known (and yes, feared) throughout the galaxy.

WHAT YOU'LL NEED

- Tablesaw
- Drill press or handheld drill
- Bench sander or orbital sander
- Bandsaw
- Square
- Block plane
- Pencil
- Spray adhesive
- Wood glue
- Gel cyanoacrylate
- Scissors
- Sandpaper (180, 240, 320 grits)
- Finish or paint(s) of your choice

- ¾ in. Forstner drill bit
- ⅜ in. brad-point drill bit
- ¼ in. brad-point drill bit
- ⅛ in. brad-point drill bit
- ³/₁₆ in. skip-tooth bandsaw blade
- Router and router table
- ¼ in. router straight bit
- 1 copy of template 1
- 2 copies of template 2
- 2 copies of template 3

MATERIALS

QTY	PART	DIMENSIONS
1	Fuselage	¾ x 1³/₁₆ x 6⅛ in.
1	Fuselage (contrasting stock)	³/₁₆ x 1³/₁₆ x 6⅛ in.
1	Fuselage	¼ x 1³/₁₆ x 6⅛ in.
1	Exhaust dowel (contrasting stock)	¾ x ¾ in.
1	Wings	¼ x 4 x 8½ in.
1	Gun housings (contrasting stock)	½ x 2 x 3⅛ in.
2	Gun dowels (contrasting stock)	1 x ¼ in.
2	Gun dowels	¾ x ⅛ in.

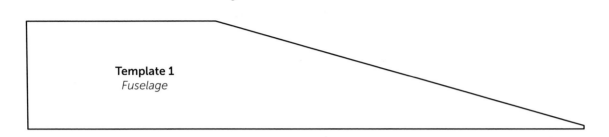

TEMPLATES: ANELEAN STARBLADE

Copy at 100%

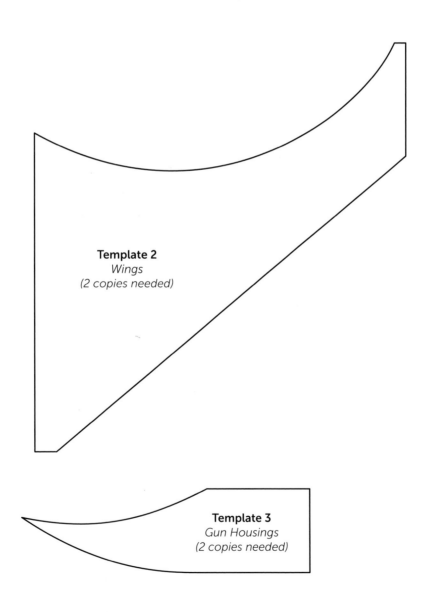

Template 1
Fuselage

Template 2
Wings
(2 copies needed)

Template 3
Gun Housings
(2 copies needed)

THE FUSELAGE

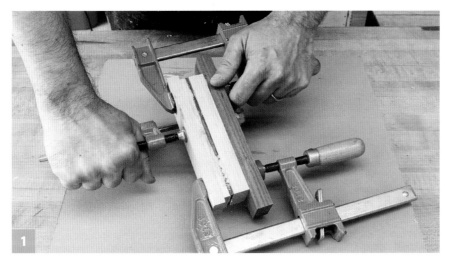

1 **Glue up the blank.** Spreading wood glue on each piece as you go, start with a ¾ x 1³⁄₁₆ x 6⅛ in. piece of stock, top it with a ³⁄₁₆ x 1³⁄₁₆ x 6⅛ in. piece of contrasting stock, and top that with a ¼ x 1³⁄₁₆ x 6⅛ in. piece that matches your first piece. Clamp and set aside to dry for three to four hours.

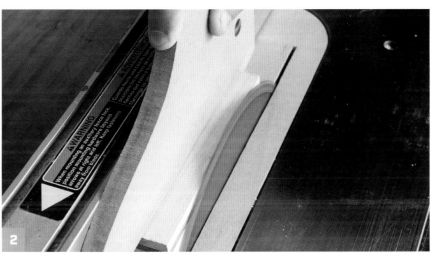

2 **Mill it to final dimension.** Plane or trim at the tablesaw to remove glue and flatten the sides that may have shifted slightly during glue-up. You're looking for a piece that's 1⅛ x 1⅛ x 6 in.

3 **Drill for the exhaust.** At the drill press, drill a centered ¾ in. hole, ¼ in. deep, into one end of the stock.

4 **Drill for the base/ hand-hold.** Drill a ⅜ in. hole centered on the underside of the fuselage (the thicker piece of light-colored wood), ⅜ in. deep.

THE FUSELAGE *(continued)*

5 Attach the exhaust pipe. Glue a ¾ in. length of ¾ in. dowel into the hole.

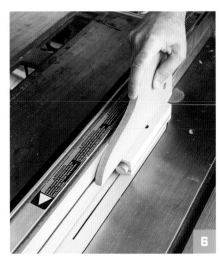

6 Add cool detail. Lower your tablesaw blade for a ¹⁄₃₂ in.-deep cut and set the fence ¼ in. from the blade. Run the piece along the fence with the top face down, then rotate it to run the opposite side against the fence and create two shallow parallel grooves that run along the "roof" of the piece.

7 Cut it out. Apply template 1 with spray adhesive so the long side is at the bottom edge. At the bandsaw, cut to the lines without going over.

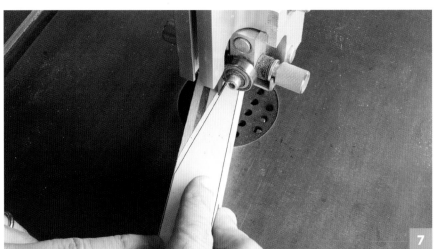

8 Cut side chamfers. Set your tablesaw blade to 10° and chamfer both sides of the piece so the sides tilt in from bottom to top. Make the cut with the bottom of the piece against the table top, guiding it with a push block.

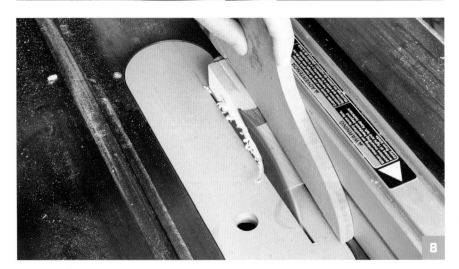

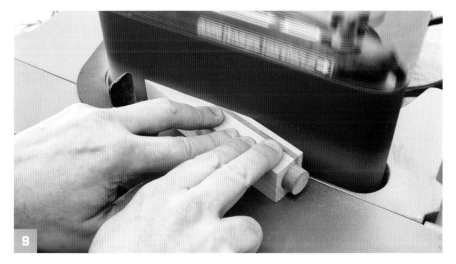

9 **Final shaping.** Smooth the piece, removing templates and bandsaw marks at the bench sander. Soften the top edges and gently round the front slope to give the cockpit a curved shape, adding slight tapers at the front corners.

THE WINGS

10 **Prep the stock.** Set your tablesaw blade for a 20° cut and chamfer one long edge of a 4 x 8½ x ¼ in. piece of stock.

11 **Apply the templates.** Cut out two copies of template 2, cutting out one of them right to the template lines. Glue them to the board, with the template cut to the lines face down, and line up the interior edges of the templates with the chamfered edge on the board.

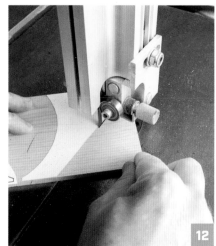

12 **Cut them out.** At the bandsaw, cut to the line/edges without going over. For best results with the tight curves, use a 3/16 in. skip-tooth blade with four teeth per inch.

13 **Time to sand.** At the bench sander, remove the bandsaw marks and the templates. Create 45° chamfers along the front and back edges of each wing, on both sides of the stock.

14 **Rout the gun housing stock.** Set up your router with a ¼ in. straight-edge bit raised ¼ in. above the surface of the table. With the fence ⅛ in. from the edge of the bit, rout a dado into the two 3⅛ in. sides of a 2 x 3⅛ piece of ½ in. stock.

15 **On to the templates.** Apply two copies of template 3 to the stock, with the inside edges (the edge toward which the curved tip points) lined up with the outer (dadoed) edges of the stock and the front ends of the templates lined up with the ends of the stock.

16 **Mark for drilling.** Make a pencil mark on each end of the stock where the front end of the templates meet the ends of the stock, ½ in. from the sides of the stock and centered across the ½ in. width.

17 **Drill the gun housings.** At the drill press, drill ¼ in. holes ¼ in. deep at each mark.

18 **Cut them out.** Cut out the housings at the bandsaw, sticking close to the lines without going over.

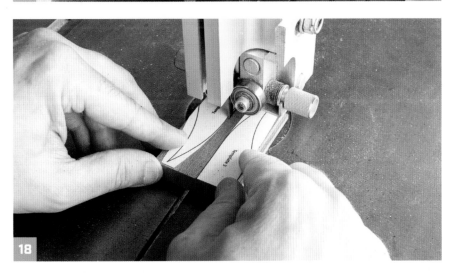

19 **Refine the pieces.** At the bench sander, smooth the edges and round the curves until you have a streamlined, smooth shape that ends in a fine point.

20 **Drill the guns.** Mark the centers on one end of each of two 1 in. lengths of ¼ in. dowel and drill ⅛ in. holes ¼ in. deep.

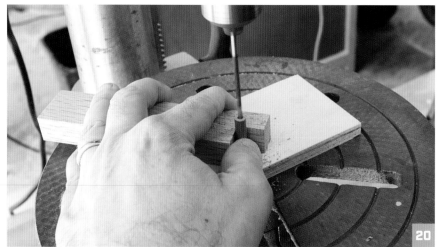

21 **Glue them up.** Glue ¾ in. lengths of ⅛ in. dowel into the holes, and then glue the completed barrel into the housing.

22 **Complete the wings.** Spread wood glue along the dadoes in the gun housings and attach them to the wings as shown.

THE FINAL BUILD

23 **Attach the wings.** Spread wood glue and a few dots of gel cyanoacrylate along the interior edges of the wings and attach them to the fuselage, positioning them parallel to and about 1/32 in. from the bottom the piece. Use a square to align them to the edge and hold them firmly in place until the glue takes hold.

24 **Finish it.** Danish oil really makes the contrasting woods on this one pop.

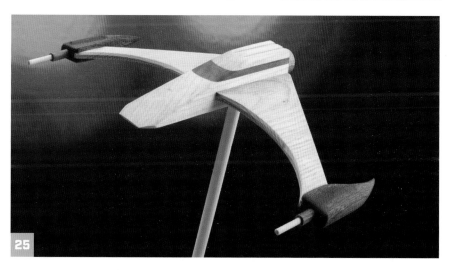

25 **Go for a sunset cruise.** Gently lift the Starblade and slowly coast, banking in a wide curve while your pilots admire the magnificent Anelean double suns, which never gets old.

12

THE DARKBLOOM

The Darkbloom came about as the result of a challenge. After looking through an early batch of designs, my friend and trusted advisor in all things science fiction and fantasy, Chris Hocking, suggested rather emphatically that what I needed was something deeply alien and fearsome, the kind of bizarre vessel that would clearly not be of human origin. Well, this one is certainly of human origin, but I think its organic lines and the Cthulhu-like tentacles give it a dose of what Chris was asking for. I leave it to you to imagine just what its crew would look like.

WHAT YOU'LL NEED

- Tablesaw
- Drill press or handheld drill
- Bench sander or orbital sander
- Bandsaw
- Square
- Block plane
- Pencil
- Spray adhesive
- Wood glue
- Gel cyanoacrylate
- Scissors
- Sandpaper (180, 240, 320 grits)
- Finish or paint(s) of your choice
- Router and router table
- $3/8$ in. router straight bit
- $3/8$ in. brad-point drill bit
- Small bar clamp
- Warm water
- Jar or can with a diameter of at least 5 in.
- Utility knife
- 4 copies of template 1
- 8 copies of template 2

MATERIALS

QTY	PART	DIMENSIONS
1	Core	1 x 1 x 6¾ in.
1	Core dowel	¾ x ⅝ in.
1	Wings	½ x 5 x 8½ in.
1	Winglets	⅛ x 1 x 19½ in.
1	Tentacles	2 x 3 x 4 in.

TEMPLATES:
THE DARKBLOOM

Copy at 100%

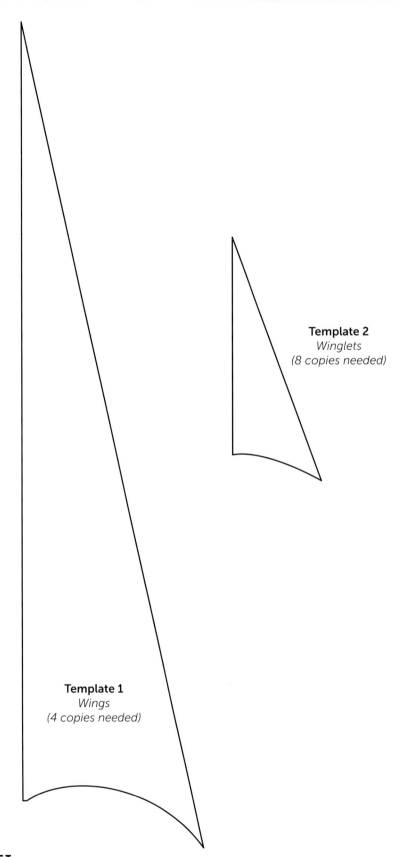

Template 2
Winglets
(8 copies needed)

Template 1
Wings
(4 copies needed)

THE CORE

1 Drill a hole. Mark the center of one end of a 1 x 1 x 6¾ in. piece of stock in the wood of your choice (if you are painting it, you don't have to be too picky). At the drill press, drill a ¾ in. hole ½ in. deep.

2 Rout dadoes for the wings. Set up your router at the router table with a ⅜ in. straight bit and adjust it for a ⅛ in. deep cut. Set your fence 5/16 in. from the edge of the bit and rout grooves end to end along all four sides of the piece.

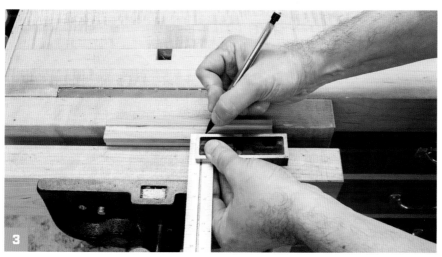

3 Chamfer the edges. Using your square as a guide, mark lines 3/16 in. from every edge. With your block plane, create a ⅜ in. wide chamfer along all four edges of the piece to create an octagonal shape.

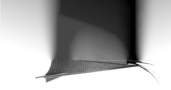

THE CORE *(continued)*

4 **Drill for the base/ hand-hold.** Drill a ³⁄₈ in. hole centered on one of the chamfered faces, ³⁄₈ in. deep.

5 **Insert a dowel.** Cut a ¾ in. length of ⅝ in. dowel and glue it into the ¾ in. hole, centering it to leave an even ⅛ in. gap between the dowel and the sides of the hole.

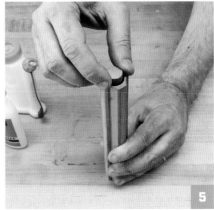

THE WINGS

6 **Apply the wing templates.** Glue four copies of template 1 to a 5 x 8½ in. piece of ½ in. stock.

7 **Cut them out.** At the bandsaw, cut to the lines without going over.

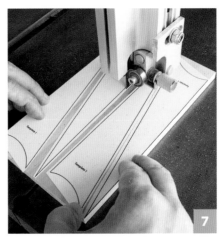

8 **Refine the wings.** At the bench sander, remove the bandsaw marks and templates and round out the curves.

9 **Chamfer the outer edges.** With a block plane or at the bench sander, create a 45° chamfer along both sides of the exterior edges, ⅛ in. wide at the back and widening to 3/16 in. at the front end.

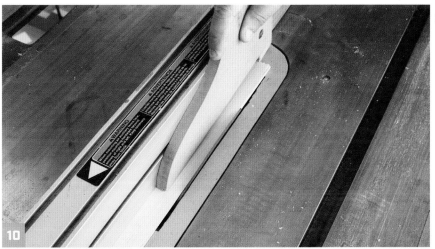

10 **Chamfer winglet stock.** Set your tablesaw blade for a 20° cut and chamfer one long edge of a 1 x 19½ in. strip of ⅛ in. stock.

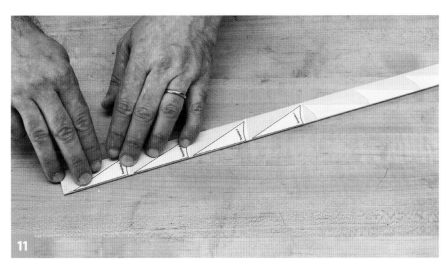

11 **Apply the winglet templates.** Make eight copies of template 2 and cut them out, with four of them cut out along the lines. Applying the templates you cut along the lines face down, line up the straight edges of the templates to the edge of the chamfered stock.

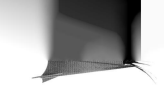

THE WINGS *(continued)*

12 **Cut them out.**
At the bandsaw, cut to the lines without going over.

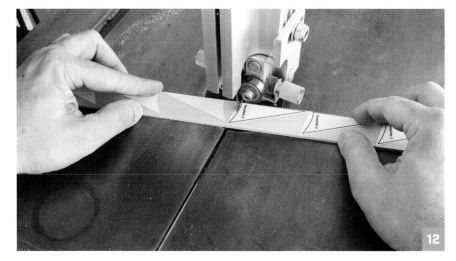

13 **Refine the winglets.**
At the bench sander, remove the bandsaw marks and templates and round out the curves, sharpening the points. Stack the pieces and clamp them together, sanding the edges all at once to ensure a consistent shape.

14 **Glue up the wings.**
Glue the winglets in pairs to the rear tips of the wings so that they're angled out from the fuselage, lining them up with the edge of the wing chamfer as shown.

THE TENTACLES

15 **Cut the veneers.** At the tablesaw, cut several thin veneers from a 2 x 3 x 4 in. block, as close as possible to $\frac{1}{32}$ in. in thickness. Advance the wood slowly to ensure an even cut and keep the veneers from tearing away.

16 **Soak the veneers.** Immerse the veneers in warm water for at least one hour.

17 **Form the veneers.** Pat the veneers dry and tape them to the side of a jar or can with a diameter of about five inches (I used a one-quart paint can), curving them lengthwise around the form. Set aside to dry overnight.

18 **Create the tentacles.** Remove the tape and set the pieces on a scrap board. Working free hand with a utility knife, cut away 15 or so tapered strips of varying lengths between 2½ and 4 inches. Move slowly and steadily to avoid snapping the thin pieces.

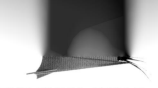

THE FINAL BUILD

19 **Attach the wings.** Spread wood glue and a few dots of gel cyanoacrylate along the interior edges of the wings and press them firmly into the dadoes. The fit should be tight enough to hold them in place until the glue sets.

20 **Paint it.** If you choose to varnish the piece, you can wait until after step 23 to do so. For an evil multi-colored paint job, spray the body with several coats of a glossy blood-red and light sprays of gloss yellow and orange, with a final splash of metallic grey that is also used to paint the tentacles.

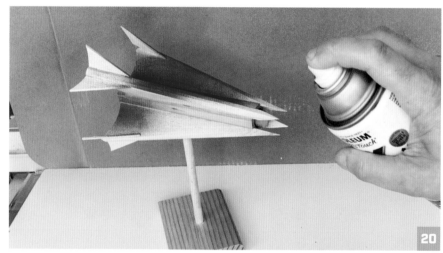

21 **Attach the tentacles.** Randomly attach the tentacles into the tip of the fuselage, dotting the ends with gel cyanoacrylate and inserting them into the gap around the dowel, holding them in place until the glue sets.

22

— DISPLAYING YOUR SHIPS —

An alternative to flying your ships into deep space at warp speed is to display them on their own stands. Drill a ³⁄₈ in. hole in the bottom of the ship's hull, before you've attached the wings or any other pieces. I like to angle the drilling, tilting the hull on the drill press table to achieve the angle I want so the finished ship will appear to be landing, taking off, or banking along a sharp curve. I vary the angles from ship to ship, so that

lined-up, the fleet looks like it's zooming this way and that. Drill another ³⁄₈ in. hole in a ¹⁄₂ in. piece of stock cut to 4 x 4 in. Once your ship is completed, attach it to the base with a ³⁄₈ in. dowel cut to the length of your choice. This same hole also provides a spot where you can insert a 3 in. dowel to create a hand-hold so you can more readily navigate the ship.

22 Terrify the good guys. Move the ship very slowly into view and have it come to a stop, where it sits in brooding silence. Tremble in fear as you gaze upon the alien horror of the Darkbloom.

THE HARBINGER

The Harbinger incorporates several of my favorite elements from other projects in this book to craft a distinctive look: the long nose echoing that of the Scout Fighter, broad wings like the Yburian Transport, and the tapered fuselage that builds on that of the Anelean Starhawk. I think the thinner wings provide a lightness that counterbalances the heft of the fuselage. Feel free to use ¼ in. plywood for the wings instead of the solid stock for a different look.

WHAT YOU'LL NEED

- Tablesaw
- Drill press or handheld drill
- Bench sander or orbital sander
- Bandsaw
- Square
- Block plane
- Pencil
- Spray adhesive
- Wood glue
- Gel cyanoacrylate
- Scissors
- Sandpaper (180, 240, 320 grits)
- Finish or paint(s) of your choice
- ⅜ in. brad-point drill bit
- 1 copy each of templates 1 and 2
- 2 copies of template 3

MATERIALS

QTY	PART	DIMENSIONS
1	Fuselage	⅞ x 1¼ x 8⅝ in.
1	Nose (contrasting stock)	⅛ x ⅜ x 11 in.
1	Cockpit (contrasting stock)	½ x 2½ x 3 in.
1	Wings	⅛ x 3³⁄₁₆ x 12 in.
2	Exhaust dowels (contrasting stock)	3 x ½ in.
2	Gun dowels	4 x ³⁄₁₆ in.

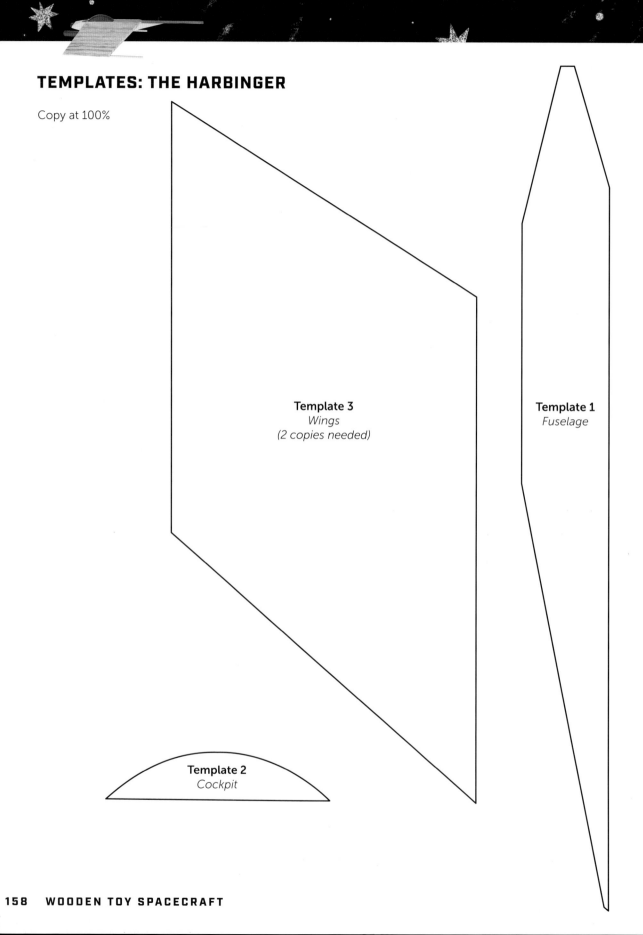

TEMPLATES: THE HARBINGER

Copy at 100%

Template 3
Wings
(2 copies needed)

Template 1
Fuselage

Template 2
Cockpit

THE FUSELAGE

1 **Drill for the base/hand-hold.** Drill a ⅜ in. hole centered on one of the 1¼ in. faces of a ⅞ x 1¼ x 8⅝ piece of stock, 3 in. from one end and ⅜ in. deep.

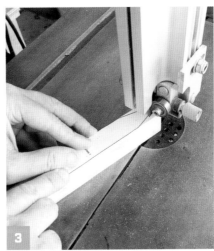

2 **Apply template.** Apply template 1 to one of the ⅞ in. faces of the stock, making sure the double-tapered end is closest to the end from which you measured the 3 in. distance in step 1 (this is the tail end).

3 **Cut it out.** At the bandsaw, cut to the lines without going over.

4 **Sand it.** At the bench sander, sand to the template lines, removing the bandsaw marks and template. Lightly round the tail end.

THE FUSELAGE *(continued)*

5 **Chamfer the sides.** Set your tablesaw blade at 45°. Adjust the fence so the cut will leave a ³⁄₈ in.-wide strip at the top of the piece and come halfway down the sides. Advance slowly and use a push stick to ensure a safe, smooth cut.

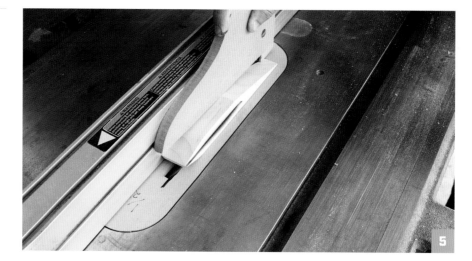

6 **Attach the top/nose piece.** Glue a ¹⁄₈ x ³⁄₈ x 11 in. strip of wood (cherry contrasts nicely with the maple of the fuselage used here) to the top of the piece with wood and gel cyanoacrylate.

7 **Refine the shape.** With a block plane, chamfer the sides of the strip to match the 45° sides of the fuselage. Support the extended nose section on a backing board to keep it from snapping off.

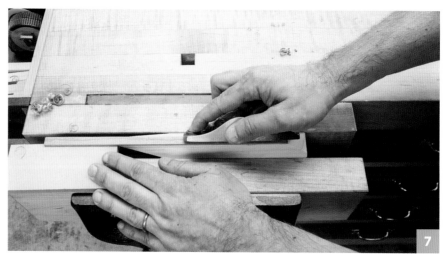

8 **Refine it a bit more.** At the bench sander, lightly chamfer the narrow back end of the strip to match the curve of the fuselage where it tapers at the tail.

THE COCKPIT

9 **Grab that template.** Attach template 2 to a 3 x 2½ in. piece of ½ in. stock, making sure the grain runs along the 2½ in. length (this is a bigger piece than you need, but allows for a safer cut at the bandsaw).

10 **Cut it out.** At the bandsaw, cut to the lines without going over. Play it safe with this small piece: hold onto the stock from the distant end as you cut and use a push stick near the end of the cut.

11 **Refine the shape.** Remove the bandsaw lines and round out the canopy shape at the bench sander. Lightly chamfer or round over (your choice) the curved edges of the pieces. Again, watch your fingers working with this small piece.

THE WINGS

12 **Apply the templates.** Glue two copies of template 3 to a 3³/₁₆ x 12 in. piece of ¹/₈ in. stock. Make sure the grain runs along the 12 in. length.

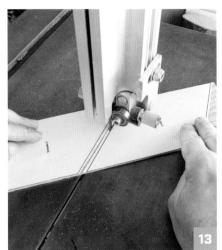

13 **Cut them out.** At the bandsaw, cut to the lines without going over.

14 **Sand them smooth.** At the bench sander, sand to the lines, removing the bandsaw marks and the templates.

15 **Chamfer the edges.** With a block plane or at the bench sander, create 30° chamfers along the front and outer edges of the wings. You can judge the angle by eye; no need to be precise about the angle so long as the chamfer is a consistent width.

16 **Attach the wings.** Glue each wing to the chamfered sides of the fuselage, aligning the interior edge of the wing to the top edge of the fuselage. There will be a slight overhang.

17 **Chamfer the top edges.** Run a block plane along the top, removing edges from the wings to create a flat surface approximately 5/16 in. wide, along the top of the fuselage.

THE FINAL BUILD

18 **Attach the cockpit.** Apply gel cyanoacrylate to the flat face of the cockpit and attach it to the top of the fuselage, 3/16 in. from the start of the curve at the back.

19 **Attach the exhaust pipes.** Spread a thin line of gel cyanoacrylate where the dowel meets the wing and the fuselage, and attach a 3 in. length of 1/2 in. dowel to each side of the fuselage at the back beneath the wing. It should extend 3/4 in. from the back end of the fuselage.

THE FINAL BUILD (continued)

20 **Attach the guns.** Cut two 4 in. lengths of ³/₁₆ in. dowel and use cyanoacrylate to glue them to the underside of each wing at the outermost edge. They should protrude 2 in. forward from the edges of the wings; align them with a straight edge. Use plenty of glue and hold it in place for a good 45 seconds until it sets.

21 **Finish it.** Apply your favorite finish or paint. Spray lacquer makes it easy to reach all the nooks of this ship.

22 **Return triumphant.**
Smoothly bring the ship in for a landing on your benchtop while simulating the massive roar of a welcoming crowd.

── **EXPANDING YOUR FLEET** ──

The 13 projects in this book are of course just a small sampling of what's possible in wooden spacecraft design. You can and should draw inspiration as I did from the long history of both factual and fictional spaceship design, along with deep contemplation of a box of wood scraps. But I'd also suggest a mix-and-match approach based on the individual elements in this book. Don't hesitate to shuffle the designs and techniques to, say, take the wings from one project and attach them to the fuselage of another. Adjust the angle of a wing, a nose, or a tail for an entirely fresh look. Attach fins, an extra set of wings, or more guns. Experiment freely, and from these 13 projects you can launch a thousand ships.

ABOUT THE AUTHOR

Gonzalo Ferreyra's day job for close to 30 years has been in various capacities in the book industry, but on weekday evenings and weekend mornings he can be found in his woodshop working on an ambitious mid-century furniture piece or tinkering to see what he can create from the fantastic cut-offs in his scrap bin. He lives in Castro Valley, California, with his wife and two small dogs, and likes to torment his two daughters by asking them to join him on a "quick" visit to the lumberyard.

DEDICATION

To Wendy, always

THANK YOU

No book is the work of one person. I want to thank Paul McGahren and Matthew Teague for "getting me" so well and guiding this project through to completion, Kerri Landis, Lindsay Hess, and Jodie Delohery for making it all beautiful, my brother Alex for helping inspire my passion for woodworking, Aaron Abrams for his fabulous video production, and MacBeath Hardwood in Berkeley for having every dowel in stock that I could possibly need. Finally, gratitude and love to Wendy, Ellie, Ruby, Gigi, and Zelda for making life wonderful and putting up with the sawdust.

METRIC CONVERSIONS

In this book, I've used inches and yards, showing anything less than one as a fraction. If you want to convert those to metric measurements, please use the following formulas:

Fractions to Decimals

⅛ = .125

¼ = .25

½ = .5

⅝ = .625

¾ = .75

Imperial to Metric Conversion: Length

Multiply inches by 25.4 to get millimeters

Multiply inches by 2.54 to get centimeters

Multiply yards by .9144 to get meters

For example, if you wanted to convert 1 ⅛ inches to millimeters: 1.125 in. x 25.4 mm = 28.575 mm

And to convert 2 ½ yards to meters: 2.5 yd. x .9144 m = 2.286 m

INDEX

MORE GREAT BOOKS *from*
SPRING HOUSE PRESS

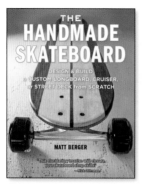

The Handmade Skateboard
978-1-940611-06-8
$24.95 | 160 Pages

Classic Wooden Toys
978-1-940611-34-1
$24.95 | 176 Pages

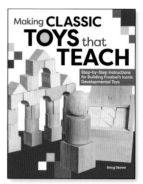

Making Classic Toys That Teach
978-1-940611-33-4
$24.95 | 144 Pages

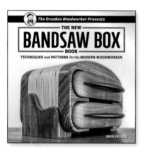

The New Bandsaw Box Book
978-1-940611-32-7
$19.95 | 120 Pages

Make Your Own Cutting Boards
978-1-940611-45-7
$22.95 | 168 Pages

Make Your Own Knife Handles
978-1-940611-53-2
$24.95 | 168 Pages

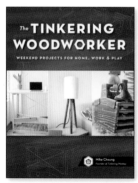

The Tinkering Woodworker
978-1-940611-08-2
$24.95 | 152 Pages

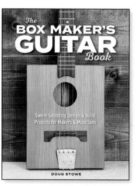

The Box Maker's Guitar Book
978-1-940611-64-8
$24.95 | 168 Pages

The Reclaimed Woodworker
978-1-940611-54-9
$24.95 | 160 Pages

SPRING HOUSE PRESS